BIRD WATCHER'S DIGEST

EASY Simple Projects to Attract & Retain the Birds You Want

BIRDHOUSES

& FEEDERS

MICHAEL BERGER

Photos and Illustrations by Michael Anderson

COOL
SPRINGS
PRESS
Growing Successful Gardeners™

First published in 2014 by Cool Springs Press,
a member of the Quayside Publishing Group,
400 First Avenue North, Suite 400, Minneapolis, MN 55401

Cool Springs Press titles are also available at discounts in bulk quantity for indus-
trial or sales-promotional use. For details write to Special Sales Manager at Cool
Springs Press, 400 First Avenue North, Suite 400, Minneapolis, MN 55401 USA.
To find out more about our books, visit us online at www.coolspringspress.com.

Library of Congress Cataloging-in-Publication Data

Berger, Michael, 1967-

  Easy birdhouses & feeders : simple projects to attract & retain the birds you
want / Michael Berger.

      pages cm. -- (Birdwatcher's digest)

  Summary: "Easy-to-build plans for making your own birdhouses and
birdfeeders. Emphasis on building and planning for bird safety"-- Provided by
publisher.

  ISBN 978-1-59186-599-5 (pbk.)

  1. Birdhouses--Design and construction. 2. Bird feeders--Design and
construction. I. Title. II. Title: Easy birdhouses and feeders.

  QL676.5.B393 2014

  728'.927--dc23

                                    2013047685

Acquisitions Editor: Mark Johanson
Design Manager: Brad Springer
Layout: S. E. Anderson
Front Cover Design: Matthew Simmons

Printed in China
10 9 8 7 6 5 4 3 2 1

The natural world is a wonder to behold, and there's no easier way to enjoy it than by attracting birds to your backyard. Not only are they beautiful and oftentimes comical to observe, but their songs are a delight to hear, and they help keep insects at bay—a true blessing when you're trying to enjoy your own piece of the great outdoors. And in order to attract our feathered friends, you need to provide three things for them: shelter, feed, and water. This book will show you how to do all three.

Building birdhouses, bird feeders, and birdbaths has been a tradition in my family for over one hundred years. My great-aunts and great-uncles built them, and they in turn taught my father to build them. And when I was old enough to hold a hammer, he taught me.

As an enthusiastic and avid birder and Boy Scout leader, I've taught many people over the years how to build ideal habitats for birds, and many are surprised at how easy it can be. These projects are great first-time projects for little hands, as you don't need any special skills or expensive tools—just a desire to attract birds to your backyard or to provide homes for species whose natural habitat has been threatened. Your reward will be the bright splash of colors as the birds you've attracted flit from home to feeder to bath.

—Michael Berger

CONTENTS

Birdhouse Basics

Birdhouses are easy to build and require neither expensive tools nor exotic woods. With just a few hand or power tools, a few types of fasteners, and some weather-resistant glue, you'll be able to quickly construct homes for your avian friends.

TOOLS

Because birdhouses are not all that complicated, you can build most of them using nothing more than simple hand tools. At a minimum, you will need a handsaw, a hand-powered drill (called a brace), a variety of drill bits, a hole saw set, a hammer, and a chisel. In addition, you'll need a tape measure, a square of some sort (to help you mark out straight cut lines), and a few clamps to aid in assembly.

Handsaw

Brace

Chisel

Hole
saw set

Hammer

To build birdhouses, at a bare minimum you'll need a hole saw set (which allows you to drill large holes from 1″ to 3″ in diameter), a hand brace and a variety of bits, a handsaw, a chisel, and a hammer.

Tape measure

Clamp

Square

You'll need a variety of clamps to help hold parts together during assembly, and you'll need a tape measure and a square to measure and lay out parts and cut lines.

A jigsaw and a drill/driver will make cutting and assembly much faster, as will bits for driving screws. Notice the bottom bit: it's a countersink bit for drilling pilot holes for screws that leave the screw head flush with the surface of the workpiece.

Drill/Driver

Drill bits

Jigsaw

While you don't absolutely *have* to own power tools to build birdhouses, they make construction much easier. Luckily, you only need two: a jigsaw and a drill/driver. If you don't own a jigsaw and would like to purchase one, choose a model that is outfitted with an adjustable cutting angle, as it will make cutting bevels (which are needed for a few of the designs in this book) substantially faster and easier.

WOOD

Birds are not picky critters; provided you've built the birdhouse according to the dimensions needed for a given species, they won't care what type of wood you've used. You should, however, use wood that's best suited for the outdoors. Species such as cedar, cypress, and redwood are naturally rot resistant and great choices for birdhouse projects. Pine, fir, and exterior-rated (or marine) plywood also are suitable choices for birdhouses, although pine and fir will not last as long as cedar.

DIMENSIONAL LUMBER SIZES	
Given size	Actual Size
1×4	¾″ × 3½″
1×6	¾″ × 5½″
1×8	¾″ × 7½″
1×10	¾″ × 9¼″
1×12	¾″ × 11¼″

When purchasing lumber for birdhouses, you'll usually buy what's known as "dimensional" lumber. Sold in sizes where the first number represents the thickness of the board and the second indicates the width, dimensional lumber is always slightly smaller than the size under which it is sold (see "Dimensional Lumber Sizes").

For pine and fir, 1× material is usually ¾″ thick. In the case of cedar, the thickness can vary depending on the provider. I've found 1× cedar that's ⅞″ thick, and I've found other examples that are ¾″ thick. *Note:* All of the dimensions in this book assume an actual thickness of ¾″.

One type of wood to avoid at all cost is pressure-treated lumber. Except as a mounting post for a birdhouse or feeder, under no circumstances should you ever use pressure-treated in your birdhouse projects. All pressure-treated lumber contains chemicals that are a deadly poison, and those chemicals can leach through eggshells and into the developing embryos.

FASTENERS AND GLUE

For all the projects in this book, you'll only need three types of fasteners: 1⅝" exterior-rated Phillips-head screws, 2" exterior-rated ring-shank nails (sometimes referred to as "maze" nails or siding nails), and nail-in electrical cable tacks.

These latter fasteners are available at most hardware stores, sold in the electrical department, and consist of a plastic strap and two small nails. Used to hold electrical cable in place, they make great catches for securing cleanout doors on birdhouses (after you remove one of the two nails).

When purchasing nails and screws, buy fasteners that are rated for exterior use. These include ones that are coated, galvanized, or made from stainless steel.

All the fasteners you need to build birdhouses are readily available at your local hardware store. Seen from left to right is a ring-shank nail, a square-head stainless steel screw, a Phillips-head galvanized screw, and a nail-in electrical cable tack (with one nail removed).

PAINTING BIRDHOUSES

Except in very specific cases, I do not paint my birdhouses, as I believe that the more natural-looking you can make the house, the better your chances will be of having a bird take up residence within. The few exceptions I make are for purple martin houses, which I usually paint white, and screech owl houses, which I usually paint or stain a dark brown.

If you opt to paint any of your houses, make sure to use paint that is exterior-rated and nontoxic, and only paint the exterior surfaces of the birdhouse. Never paint the inside edges of the entrance hole or the inside of the box itself.

When it comes to adhesives, I only use two types of glue: waterproof wood glue and polyurethane glue. Waterproof wood glue has been around for years, is easy to work with, and is easy to clean up. Polyurethane glue is exceptionally strong. It's great for filling gaps, as it foams and expands as it cures. It is, however, more difficult to clean up if you spill a bit, and you'll need to lightly dampen your workpieces with water before applying the glue.

Any glue that is rated for exterior use should be fine to use for birdhouse construction. A few of my favorites include Titebond III wood glue, Gorilla wood glue, and Gorilla polyurethane glue.

PREDATOR GUARDS

Because bird nests are extremely vulnerable to predators such as raccoons, snakes, squirrels, and other birds, it's important to give as much protection as possible for your houses' residents. There are many different designs of predator guards, but four that I have found to work the best are a baffle block, a metal guard, a wire guard, and a baffle-style guard.

A baffle block (*at right*) is nothing more than a block of wood with a hole drilled through it that forms an extension of the entrance hole. The extra depth that the baffle block creates makes it difficult for raccoons to reach in and grab eggs or nestlings.

A metal guard (*page 12*) is merely a sheet of metal with an appropriately sized hole cut in it. The sheet mounts on the front face of the birdhouse and prevents gnawing predators, such as squirrels, or pecking birds, such as starlings or sparrows, from enlarging the hole and gaining access to the inside.

One of the most successful types of predator guards is the baffle-style guard (*page 12*). Built to go around a length of conduit that serves as the birdhouse's mounting pole, this type of guard does an exceptional job of keeping climbing predators from scaling the pole and getting to the birdhouse.

To build this type of guard, you'll need a 5-foot length of ½″-dia. metal conduit, a 5-foot length of #4 iron rebar, a 34-inch length of 7″-dia. stovepipe, a small radiator hose clamp, and a 10″ × 10″ piece of 1″-thick lumber. First assemble the stovepipe. Usually sold flat, you'll need to interlock the seam that turns it into

MONITORING AND CLEANING BIRDHOUSES

To ensure that your feathered friends have the best nesting success, monitor the houses during nesting season by following these tips:

- Examine the nest once or twice a week at midday.

- Knock on the house and whistle loudly before opening it.

- Avoid handling eggs or nestlings.

- Keep track of when eggs are laid or hatch.

- Learn to recognize nests and eggs. Because house sparrows are considered a nuisance species, you may legally remove their nests and eggs.

When nesting season ends, clean out your houses. Wearing gloves and a dust mask, open the house and remove all old nesting materials. Clean out drainage holes, and then disinfect the box with a 10 percent bleach spray and allow to dry. Come spring, check the houses again to make sure that unwanted critters did not move in during the winter.

For additional resources on cleaning and monitoring, please see the Bird Watcher's Digest website, found in the Resources Guide on page 158.
For a form to help you record your schedules and comments, see page 159.

A baffle block attached to the front of a birdhouse adds extra depth to the entrance hole and makes it difficult for predators to reach the eggs or nestlings within the box.

When adding a sheet metal predator guard, use decorative metal such as copper to enhance the appearance of the birdhouse. The ring keeps chewing and clawing predators from enlarging the hole to gain access.

a round pipe. Once joined, use it as a template to trace and cut out a circle of wood from your 10″-square scrap; then mark the center of the wood circle and drill at that point a ⅝″-dia. hole. Insert the wood circle into the stovepipe so that it is flush with the top and drive 1″ screws through the stovepipe wall and into the wood, securing it in place.

To install the guard, start by driving the 5-foot length of rebar halfway into the ground at the location where you want to install the bird-house. Place the ½″-dia. × 5-foot conduit over the rebar. Attach the radiator clamp to the conduit at the height where you want the baffle to rest; then slip the baffle down over the conduit until it sits atop the clamp and finally use ½″ conduit straps to attach the birdhouse to the conduit mounting pole.

Predator guards such as the Gilbertson-style baffle prevent predators from climbing the pole and gaining access to the birdhouse.

A baffle-style guard consists of a wood circle that's screwed inside the top of a length of stovepipe. A radiator hose clamp attached to the birdhouse's mounting pole holds the baffle at the desired height and allows it to spin if a predator attempts to climb it.

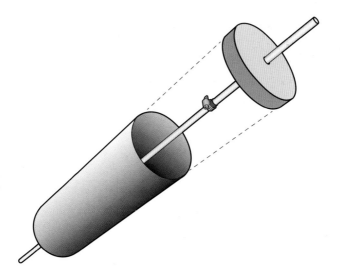

This baffle-style predator guard spins on the conduit pole, preventing climbing. It is the type of guard recommended by BirdWatcher's Digest Magazine.

BUILDING FOR BIRDS

NOTICE: *If you live in a region or neighborhood where predation is a concern, incorporate a suitable predator guard into your plans. See pages 10 to 13.*

American Robin Nesting Shelf

For many, the American Robin is the first official bird of spring, despite the fact that robins often don't migrate at all, provided they have enough food and cover to protect them from winter's chill. Nevertheless, as a child I would always look forward to the day each year when I saw my first "returning" robin, even after I had learned that many species such as the Red-winged Blackbird return earlier than the migrating robins.

This basic nesting shelf is easy to build and is the perfect project with which to introduce young hands to working with tools. While I used some scrap redwood for my version, you can use just about any weather-resistant wood species.

The American Robin is one of the most recognizable, most common, and widely distributed birds in North America.

VITAL STATISTICS

AMERICAN ROBIN (*Turdus migratorius*)

Size: 10″

Number of eggs: 3 to 7

Length of incubation: 12–14 days

Broods per season: 2–3 in south, fewer in north

Food: earthworms, insects, and berries

Range: summer, all of United States and north through Canada; winter, most of continental United States, south to Mexico

ABOUT THE BIRD

The American Robin is one of the most recognized birds in North America, and it was originally named by British colonists because of its similarity to the robin of their homeland of England.

The American Robin is a member of the thrush family. The male is olive-gray, with a black head and back, a white streaked chin and throat, and reddish-orange breast and underparts. The female, in comparison, has duller hues, and the juveniles are dark on top, much like their parents, but their but their upper wings and rumps are streaked with white, giving them a speckled appearance.

The American Robin migrates in colder climates, while in areas with a temperate winter they are often year-round residents. They often live and nest quite close to human habitation, and males stake out their territories before the females arrive.

From early fall until spring, the males do not sing; instead, they chatter and call. But come early spring, the males belt out their songs to attract a mate.

HOUSE PLACEMENT

Robins are not choosy about where they build a nest, and often will pick spots very close to people (such as in window sills, behind porch lamps, or in nearby shrubs). But for best results, follow these guidelines:

- Choose a spot that's not too close to a door or other high-traffic area.

- Pick a spot that is protected from storms and prevailing winds.

- Do not place the house too high up. Though you run a risk of higher predation, it's important to not have the nest so high that the fledglings would get hurt as they flutter out of the nest to the ground.

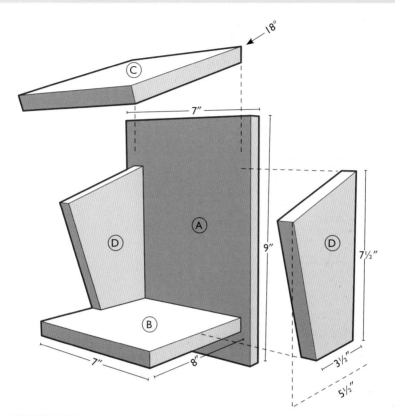

CUTTING LIST

Key	Quan.	Part	Stock	Thickness	Width	Length	Comments
A	1	Back	1×10	¾	7	9	
B	1	Floor	1×10	¾	7	8	
C	1	Roof	1×10	¾	7	8	Cut back edge at 18°
D*	2	Sides	1×10	¾	5½	7½	

*Rough dimensions; see illustration for final dimensions

HARDWARE & SUPPLIES NEEDED

1×10 × 3-ft. board	1⅝″ galvanized wood screws or 2″ galvanized ring-shank nails	Waterproof wood glue

Choose a location that's close to low-lying shrubs or other protective vegetation; once the fledglings have made their crash landing, they need cover in which to hide for a few days while they are fed by the parents.

BUILDING THE PLATFORM

1. Cut all the parts to size as indicated by the cutting list. When cutting the roof, bevel its back edge at 18° so that it rests flush on top of the sides and tight against the back.

2. Use 1⅝" exterior-rated screws and wood glue to attach the floor to the bottom edges of the sides, drilling countersunk pilot holes for each screw.

3. Attach the roof to the top of the sides, again using 1⅝" screws and wood glue. Orient the roof so that its beveled edge is flush with the back edge of the sides.

4. Glue and screw the back to the assembly. Once the glue has dried, mount the house following the House Placement tips.

After you've attached the sides to the floor, glue and screw the roof to the sides. Remember to countersink the screws so that they are flush with the surface of the roof.

Once the glue has dried, mount the platform in a sheltered location that's protected from prevailing weather.

NOTICE: If you live in a region or neighborhood where predation is a concern, incorporate a suitable predator guard into your plans. *See pages 10 to 13.*

Mourning Dove Nesting Shelf

As a child growing up in rural Ohio, I quickly became familiar with this ubiquitous bird. My mother, a Kentucky farm girl, called them "rain crows" and told me stories about how the Mourning Dove's plaintive call signaled the coming of rain. For me, the Mourning Dove was a great chance to practice my early birding skills, as I would go from one pine tree to another on our property, counting the dove nests that I could spot.

This is a variation of the open nesting platform, even easier to build and simpler in construction. Other species such as robins and some swallows will also use this open platform.

Mourning Doves can be distinguished from other dove species by their long, pointed tail bordered by large, white tips on all the feathers except for the four innermost.

VITAL STATISTICS
MOURNING DOVE (Zenaida macroura)

Size: 12″	
Number of eggs: 2	
Length of incubation: 14 days	
Broods per season: 5–6 in the South; 2–3 elsewhere	
Food: Seeds	
Range: all of Continental United States year-round, north into Canada in summer	

ABOUT THE BIRD

A graceful, slender-tailed bird, the Mourning Dove is common across the continent, and in some states is hunted as a game bird. It is easily identifiable by its small, pinkish head, olive-gray body, brownish-gray wings with black spots on the inner wing surfaces, and white tips on its outer tail feathers.

According to some researchers, Mourning Doves may mate for life, and the males will aggressively defend territories. After breeding season, however, Mourning Doves gather together to roost in sheltered groves.

An unusual behavior of Mourning Doves is that, unlike other birds, they do not lift their heads to swallow water; instead, they have the ability to suck up water from drinking pools.

Their nests consist of flimsy platforms of sticks and twigs gathered by the male but built by the female. And once the eggs hatch, the young are fed by both parents a substance called "Pigeon's milk," a regurgitated conglomeration of seeds and fluids created in the crop of the adults.

HOUSE PLACEMENT

Like robins, Mourning Doves are not particularly picky in their nesting sites; however, they do prefer more cover and often choose pine trees or other dense areas. For best results, follow these guidelines when placing your nesting platform:

- Place the nesting platform 6–12 feet off the ground.

- Pick a site that is close to, or amidst, dense trees such as pines.

- Place the nesting shelf so that it is protected from prevailing winds or bad weather.

- Choose a site that is close to small sticks or pine debris, or scatter some on the ground close to the nesting platform.

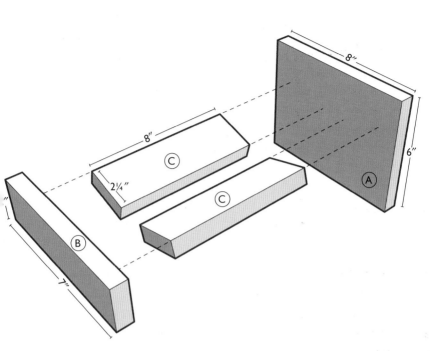

CUTTING LIST

Key	Quan.	Part	Stock	Thickness	Width	Length	Comments
A	1	Back	1×8	¾	6	8	
B	1	Front	1×8	¾	2	7	
C	2	Struts	1×8	¾	2¼	8	

HARDWARE & SUPPLIES NEEDED

1 × 8 × 3-ft. board   2″ galvanized ring-shank nails   Waterproof wood glue
1⅝″ galvanized wood screws

- Scatter seeds, particularly millet, on the ground near the nesting platform.

- Keep a sharp eye for ground predators such as cats, as mourning doves spend a significant time feeding and caring for their young on the ground.

BUILDING THE PLATFORM

1. Cut all the parts to the dimension listed in the cutting list.

2. Use glue and 1⅝″ exterior-rated screws to attach the two struts to the back. Position the struts as shown in the drawing.

3. Use glue and 2″ galvanized ring-shank nails to attach the front to the front faces of the struts.

Because cedar has a tendency to split, drill countersunk pilot holes for each screw.

Because of their soft nature, ring-shank nails have a tendency to bend. To prevent this from happening, drill pilot holes for each nail.

NOTICE: If you live in a region
or neighborhood where predation
is a concern, incorporate a suitable
predator guard into your plans.
See pages 10 to 13.

Flowerpot Nesting House

Birds are ingenious little creatures, and many are not picky about what they build a house in. I've seen wrens build houses in discarded watering cans, robins on top of old wheelbarrows, and sparrows just about anywhere you'd rather they didn't.

This house takes advantage of that tendency and can be used by a variety of small songbird species. Consisting of nothing more than a clay flowerpot and a semi-circle of wood, the flowerpot house is extremely easy to build and provides a nice bit of shelter when tucked into a tree's forking branches or mounted in any sheltered location.

HOUSE PLACEMENT

When mounting the house, you can use a wood screw and a large fender washer driven through the drainage hole at the base of the pot (which now serves as the back of the house).

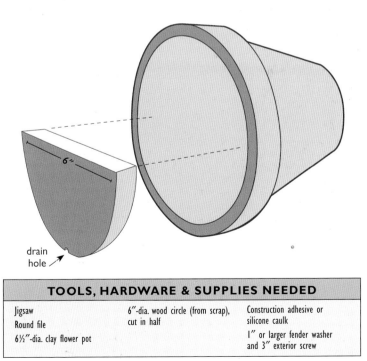

6″

drain
hole

TOOLS, HARDWARE & SUPPLIES NEEDED

Jigsaw	6″-dia. wood circle (from scrap),	Construction adhesive or
Round file	cut in half	silicone caulk
6½″-dia. clay flower pot		1″ or larger fender washer
		and 3″ exterior screw

Groove

Notice the groove in the bottom of the wood semicircular front that allows water to drain from the birdhouse. Use a round file to rasp the groove into the bottom of the front.

Attach the nesting house directly to a tree trunk using a large fender washer and a 3″ exterior screw (coarse thread).

BUILDING THE BOX

1. Measure the inside diameter of the opening of your flowerpot; then draw a circle of that diameter on a scrap of cedar and use your jigsaw to cut it out. For a 6½″-dia. flowerpot like I used, your circle should be roughly 6″ in diameter.

2. Cut the wood circle in half; then use a round file to rasp a drain hole along the bottom curve of the semicircle.

3. Use silicone caulk or construction adhesive to glue the wood semicircle into the opening of the flowerpot.

4. To mount the flowerpot birdhouse on a tree trunk, slide a 1″ or larger fender washer over a 3″ screw; then drive the screw through the drainage hole in the bottom of the flowerpot and into the tree.

NOTICE: If you live in a region or neighborhood where predation is a concern, incorporate a suitable predator guard into your plans. See pages 10 to 13.

House Wren Nesting Box

The House Wren is responsible for my love of building birdhouses. When I was six or seven years old, a coworker of my father by the name of George McElroy gave me my very first birdhouse. It was made from a small Crisco can covered in tree bark and outfitted with a conical roof and an eye screw for hanging. For many years that whimsical house always had a resident wren, and I delighted in watching the comical antics of this little bird as it came and went.

With its basic box design, this birdhouse is easy to construct, and it's the perfect "next step" project for children to tackle after having built the open nesting shelves. It incorporates a pivoting swing-out side that not only makes monitoring and cleaning out nests easy, but also provides for great nest box ventilation.

The House Wren sings a beautiful, trilling flutelike song, often cocking its tail up while it perches and calls out its melody.

VITAL STATISTICS

HOUSE WREN (*Troglodytes aedon*)

Size: 4.75″
Number of eggs: 5–9
Length of incubation: 13–15 days
Broods per season: 2–3
Food: insects, spiders, millipedes, and some snails
Range: summer, most of United States north into Canada; winter, south coastal United States south into Mexico

ABOUT THE BIRD

Besides the common House Wren, there are two other common wren species: the Carolina Wren and Bewick's Wren, and the ranges of all three species somewhat overlap. The Carolina Wren is found east of the Mississippi, while Bewick's Wren is found primarily in the South and Southwest regions of the United States.

Wrens are not that picky in their nesting site locations, and these very social, energetic birds are not shy around people. In fact, it's common for wrens to chase people away from their nesting areas when they are staking out their territory and once the eggs are laid.

When establishing territory, wrens will often invade the nests of other wrens and songbirds, puncturing their eggs and killing their young. They will also build several dummy nests, and it's not until the female picks the one she likes the best that the male will then complete one.

HOUSE PLACEMENT

Because wrens are not as picky as other species of birds, house placement is less critical than with other species. Semi-open habitats are best, with trees or shrubs nearby. For best results, follow these placement guidelines:

- Mount the house 4–10 feet off the ground.

- Locate the box close to a shrubby area.

- Choose a site that is more sunny than shady.

- Old fencerows make great mounting locations.

- Unlike other birds, wrens do not mind a house that hangs, so feel free to hang the house from a tree branch if you prefer.

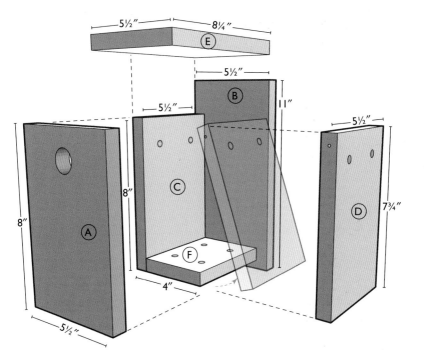

CUTTING LIST

Key	Quan.	Part	Stock	Thickness	Width	Length	Comments
A	1	Front	1×6	¾	5½	8	Center a 1⅛" hole 6½" from bottom
B	1	Back	1×6	¾	5½	11	
C	1	Side	1×6	¾	5½	8	
D	1	Side	1×6	¾	5½	7¾	
E	1	Roof	1×6	¾	5½	8¼	
F	1	Floor	1×6	¾	4	5½	Drill four ¼" drainage holes

HARDWARE & SUPPLIES NEEDED

1 × 6 × 6-ft. board
1⅝" galvanized wood screws

2" galvanized ring-shank nails
Nail-in electrical cable tack

Waterproof wood glue

BUILDING THE BOX

1. Cut all the parts to the dimensions shown in the cutting list.

2. Use a hole saw to drill a 1⅛″-dia. entrance hole in the front. Center the hole 6½″ from the bottom edge of the front. *Note:* If you don't have a hole saw, a Forstner bit will also work.

One of the easiest ways to drill entrance holes is with a hole saw. Sold as a kit, it can usually accommodate holes up to 3″ in diameter.

3. Drill four ¼″ drainage holes in the floor.

4. Use waterproof glue and either screws or nails to attach the longer of the two sides to the inside face of the front; then attach that same side to the inside face of the back.

5. Glue and screw the floor to the inside of the box; then attach the roof to the box in the same fashion.

6. To correctly attach the shorter swing-out side, position it in place so that it is flush with the bottom edge of the box. Drive two 2″ ring-shank nails, one on each side, to serve as pivot points for the swing-out side.

7. Remove one nail from a nail-in electrical cable tack; then nail the cable tack to the side edge of the front near the bottom to serve as a latch that keeps the swing-out side closed.

Clamp and attach the front to the longer of the two sides using glue and either exterior-rated ring-shank nails or screws.

NOTICE: *If you live in a region or neighborhood where predation is a concern, incorporate a suitable predator guard into your plans. See pages 10 to 13.*

Black-Capped Chickadee Nesting Box

A common visitor to bird feeding stations in the northern United States and most of Canada, for me, the chickadee signals winter and snow. Even though the bird is extremely prevalent in summer (and in fact doesn't generally migrate), it's in the winter around my bird feeders where I hear them singing their long drawn-out *chick-a-dee-dee-dee* call.

While this house (which the Carolina Chickadee in the South will also use) may look a bit more complicated than a basic box-style house, it's actually fairly basic to build provided you have a jigsaw. Because you can change the angle of the jigsaw's blade, the tool makes it easy to make the 45° cuts that this house requires.

Chickadees are quite tame, and it's not uncommon for them to eat sunflower seed out of your hand, provided you are patient and remain still.

VITAL STATISTICS

BLACK-CAPPED CHICKADEE
(*Poecile atricapilla*)

Size: 5.5″
Number of eggs: 5–10
Length of incubation: 11–13
Broods per season: 1
Food: insects, berries, and seeds
Range: year-round in the northern half of the United States and most of Canada

ABOUT THE BIRD

Chickadees, both the Black-capped and the Carolina, are vocal, energetic birds, and we've all probably heard their familiar *chick-a-dee* call. But their loud voices do not match their size; the average chickadee weighs a mere .4 ounces, equivalent to the combined weight of a quarter, nickel, and dime. They are readily seen around bird feeders and have specialized leg muscles that enable them to hang upside down.

The Black-capped Chickadee prefers deciduous and mixed deciduous-coniferous woodlands, but it is also found in suburban areas as long as there is suitable nesting sites and adequate food. They gather in flocks and have a pecking order in that a main pair will dominate over all other individuals.

During winter, chickadees have an amazing ability to enter a state of "controlled hypothermia" on cold nights, and they can drop their body temperature by 18–22° Fahrenheit to conserve energy during the night.

HOUSE PLACEMENT

Chickadees prefer to nest along forest edges and are especially prevalent along the edges of farm fields where forested areas have been disturbed. With that in mind, follow these guidelines for best house placement:

- Mount the house 4–15 feet above the ground.

- Choose a location that receives sunlight 40–60 percent of the day.

- Locate the house along edges of forests or other heavily treed areas.

- Place about 1 inch of wood chips or shavings in the bottom of the box.

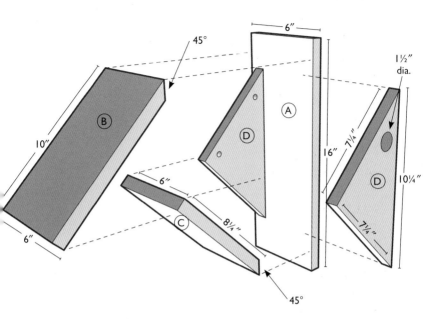

CUTTING LIST

Key	Quan.	Part	Stock	Thickness	Width	Length	Comments
A	1	Back	1×12	¾	6	16	
B	1	Roof	1×12	¾	6	10	Cut top edge at 45°
C	1	Floor	1×12	¾	6	8¼	Cut bottom edge at 45°
D	2	Sides	1×12	¾	7¼	10¼	

HARDWARE & SUPPLIES NEEDED

1×12 × 6-ft. board	1⅝″ galvanized wood screws or 2″ galvanized ring-shank nails	Waterproof wood glue

Hold a combination square tightly to the workpiece to serve as a straight edge as you make the 45° beveled cuts needed for the roof and floor.

After attaching the sides to the back, glue and screw the roof to the sides and back, followed by the floor.

BUILDING THE BOX

1. Cut the parts to the dimensions listed in the cutting list. An easy way to cut the 45° bevels along the top edge of the roof and along the bottom edge of the floor is to first set the blade angle of your jigsaw to 45°. Use a combination square as a guide to help you steady the jigsaw as you cut, and work slowly across the board, letting the saw do the work.

2. Use a hole saw or a Forstner bit to bore a 1½"-dia. entrance hole in one of the sides.

3. Use glue and 1⅝" exterior-rated screws to attach the sides flush to the edges of the back; then fasten the roof and floor to the sides and back in the same fashion. 🏠

Tufted Titmouse Nesting Box

A familiar visitor to backyards, the Tufted Titmouse is a brazen little bird, unfazed by humans. In fact, it's been known to sometimes swoop down and pluck out a human hair to use for its nest. And like the chickadee, it's quite intelligent and can also learn to eat food out of a human hand.

This birdhouse (which can also serve as a home for nuthatches) is similar in construction style to the wren house.

With its tufted gray head and rust-colored patches on its sides and flanks, the Tufted Titmouse is easy to identify.

VITAL STATISTICS
TUFTED TITMOUSE (*Baeolophus bicolor*)

Size: 6.5″	
Number of eggs: 4–8	
Length of incubation: 13–14 days	
Broods per season: 1 (occasionally 2 in south)	
Food: insects, berries, spiders, nuts, seeds	
Range: year-round in eastern half of the United States and southwest into Texas	

ABOUT THE BIRD

The Tufted Titmouse is a curious bird, just as social as the chickadee. It's a common visitor to feeders in the fall and winter, and it can be recognized by the gray feathers on its back and its gray crest, which can be either erected or laid flat.

A year-round resident, the Tufted Titmouse has expanded its range over the past 50 years. It prefers deciduous forests, swamps, orchards, parks, and suburban areas, but deforestation has taken its toll on this inquisitive species.

Titmice will cache food during the winter. You may notice as you watch your bird feeders that a titmouse will fly in and remove just one seed, flying away to a nearby tree. The bird will then shell the seed and tuck it in a crevice of a branch or in the bark of the tree trunk for consumption later.

In the spring, the male titmouse will begin feeding his mate from the time the pair begin to scout out locations for a nest. He will continue feeding her throughout the nesting period and will share in the feeding of the nestlings; in fact, some research indicates that the young from a previous brood will also assist in the feeding of the current young.

HOUSE PLACEMENT

Titmice prefer areas that have tall vegetation and mature trees with a dense canopy. And while they prefer to nest in natural tree cavities, the loss of habitat has made this difficult in some areas. For the best chance of success for your titmouse nesting box, follow these guidelines:

- Choose a location in a semishaded area on a tree or fence post.

- Mount the birdhouse 5–15 feet above the ground.

- If possible, pick a location that is a mixture of trees and open spaces.

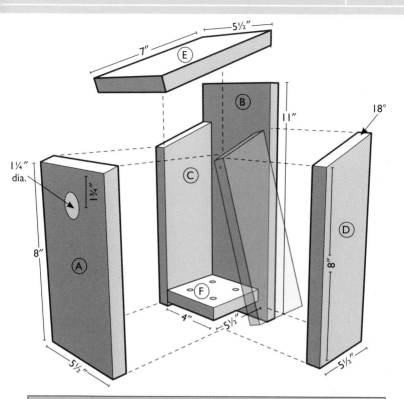

CUTTING LIST

Key	Quan.	Part	Stock	Thickness	Width	Length	Comments
A	1	Front	1×6	¾	5½	8	Center a 1¼" hole 1¾" from the top
B	1	Back	1×6	¾	5½	11	
C	1	Side	1×6	¾	5½	8	
D	1	Side	1×6	¾	5½	8	
E	1	Roof	1×6	¾	5½	7	
F	1	Floor	1×6	¾	4	5½	Drill four ¼" drainage holes

HARDWARE & SUPPLIES NEEDED

1×6 × 6-ft. board   2" galvanized ring-shank nails   Waterproof wood glue
1⅝" galvanized wood screws   Nail-in electrical cable tack

After you've attached the roof to the front and long side, glue and screw the assembly to the back.

- Place nesting materials such as hair, fur, or feathers that are no more than 3–4 inches in length near the birdhouse.

- Watch that wrens do not invade the house, especially with houses placed lower to the ground near shrubby areas.

BUILDING THE BOX

1. Cut all the parts to the dimensions shown in the cutting list.

2. Use a hole saw to drill a 1¼″-dia. entrance hole in the front centered 1¾″ from the top edge. *Note:* If you don't have a hole saw, a Forstner bit will also work.

3. Drill four ¼″ drainage holes in the floor.

A nail-in electrical cable tack (with one of its two nails removed) makes the perfect latch for keeping the swing-out inspection side closed.

4. Use waterproof glue and either screws or nails to attach the longer of the two sides to the inside face of the front; then attach the roof to the front and side in the same fashion.

5. Glue and screw the back to the birdhouse assembly; then glue and screw the floor to the inside of the box.

6. To correctly attach the shorter swing-out side, position it in place so that it is flush with the bottom edge of the box. Drive two 2″ ring-shank nails, one on each side, to serve as pivot points for the swing-out side.

7. Remove one nail from a nail-in electrical cable tack; then nail the cable tack to the side edge of the front near the bottom to serve as a latch that keeps the swing-out side closed.

NOTICE: If you live in a region or neighborhood where predation is a concern, incorporate a suitable predator guard into your plans. See pages 10 to 13.

Eastern Bluebird Nesting Box

There was a time not that long ago when you would have been truly lucky to see a bluebird, as overuse of pesticides, destruction of natural nesting habitat, and a few terrible winters had taken their toll on these colorful creatures. But thanks to the introduction of regulations on pesticides and an aggressive nationwide effort to build nesting boxes, bluebird populations have rebounded and it's no longer unusual to see these delightful birds diving down to the ground for insects.

This Eastern Bluebird nesting box (which is also acceptable for Mountain and Western Bluebirds) is based on a traditional design that incorporates a removable top for inspection and cleaning. It's easy to build—just make sure to include some type of predator guard (see pages 10 to 13 for predator guard information), such as the copper ring around the entrance hole, to keep squirrels and other gnawing critters from enlarging the opening.

Not to be confused with the Indigo Bunting (which is almost completely blue), the Eastern Bluebird sports a reddish brown breast, throat, and neck.

VITAL STATISTICS

EASTERN BLUEBIRD (*Sialia sialis*)

Size: 7.5″
Number of eggs: 2–7
Length of incubation: 14 days
Broods per season: 2–3
Food: insects, earthworms, spiders (berries and seeds in winter)
Range: summer, eastern half of United States west to the Rockies and north into lower Canada; winter, southeastern United States and south into northern Mexico

ABOUT THE BIRD

Like the American Robin, the Eastern Bluebird is a member of the thrush family. But unlike robins, bluebirds nest almost exclusively in rotting trees or in cavities made by other birds, such as abandoned woodpecker holes.

Bluebirds are migratory and fly north in the early spring, tending to return to the same area in which they previously nested. (If this is their first return, they will usually choose a site close to where they originally hatched.) The males return first to stake out their territories, and the females arrive shortly thereafter.

Once the eggs are laid, incubation lasts approximately 12–14 days for Eastern Bluebirds and 13–14 days for both Mountain and Western varieties. The female remains on the nest up to four days after hatching, as the newly hatched bluebirds are incapable of producing their own body heat. But after that, both the mother and father share in the feeding duties. After hatching, the chicks will remain in the nest for 16–22 days for Eastern, 17–22 for Mountain, and 19–22 days for Western Bluebirds.

Once the fledglings leave the nest, the father usually stays close by and continues to feed the young for several more weeks until they are strong enough to fend for themselves. The mother will start a new brood as soon as two weeks after fledge day.

HOUSE PLACEMENT

Bluebirds require semiopen land such as rural environments; because of that, suburban house placement may not be ideal. Generally, areas where there is at least an acre of open land will provide the most acceptable house sites. Grass and hayfields, meadows, lawns, or old apple orchards make the best locations. Fence-rows are also ideal provided proper steps are taken to keep predators out of the nesting boxes. For best results, follow these tips when placing your bluebird house:

- Mount the nest box 4 to 5 feet above ground.

- Face the box away from prevailing winds.

- In hot climates, face the box to the north or east to avoid direct midday sun.

- Face the box toward some tree or shrub within 100 feet so that when the young leave the nest they will make an initial flight to safety.

- Because bluebirds hunt insects by scanning the ground from a perch, spotting an insect, then swooping down to the ground to get it, try to place the box within close proximity of young trees or shrubs, fence posts, and or lower branches of a lone mature tree that might make good hunting perches.

- Place the nesting box at least 100 feet from brushy or wooded areas where wrens are likely to be, and preferably at least ¼ mile from farmyards or barns where sparrows live.

- Because bluebirds are territorial when breeding and will claim territories of 2–3 acres, they will generally not nest closer than 100 yards from the next box.

- To keep swallows out, pair boxes 5–15 feet apart. That way, swallows will only take up residence in one box, leaving the other open for the bluebirds.

BUILDING THE BOX

1. Cut all the parts according to the dimensions shown in the cutting list. An easy way to cut the 18° bevel along the back edge of the roof is to first set the blade angle of your jigsaw to 18°. Use a combination square as a guide to help you steady the jigsaw as you cut, and work slowly across the board, letting the saw do the work.

2. Drill a 1½″-dia. entrance hole centered 1¾″ from the top edge of the front. *Note:* For Western and Mountain Bluebirds, bore a 1⁹⁄₁₆″ entrance hole.

3. Drill two ¼″-dia. holes for ventilation near the top edge of each side.

4. Use glue and 1⅝″ exterior-rated screws to attach the sides flush to the inside face of the front. Note that this house does not use a swing-out side; instead, remove the top when you need to clean and inspect the birdhouse.

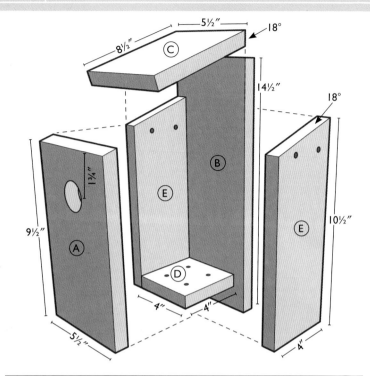

CUTTING LIST

Key	Quan.	Part	Stock	Thickness	Width	Length	Comments
A	1	Front	1×6	¾	5½	9½	Center a 1½" hole** 1¾" from top
B	1	Back	1×6	¾	5½	14½	
C	1	Roof	1×6	¾	5½	8½	Bevel top edge at 18° angle
D	1	Floor	1×6	¾	4	4	Drill four ¼" holes for drainage
E	2	Sides*	1×6	¾	4	10½	Cut top of side at 18° angle

*Rough dimensions; see illustration for final dimensions
**Mountain bluebirds require a hole that is 1⁹⁄₁₆" in diameter.

HARDWARE & SUPPLIES NEEDED

1×6 × 6-ft. board	1⁵⁄₈" galvanized wood screws	Waterproof wood glue

*Hold a combination square tightly to the workpiece to serve as a straight edge as you make the 18°
beveled cut needed for the back edge of the roof.*

5. Glue and screw the birdhouse assembly
   to the back.

6. Drill four ¼″-dia. holes in the floor for
   drainage; then glue and screw the floor
   in place.

7. Lastly, use screws to attach the roof.
   Do not use glue, as you'll need to
   periodically remove the roof for
   cleaning and inspection.

*While the Eastern Bluebird needs a
1½″-dia. entrance hole, the Western and
Mountain Bluebirds need a 1⁹⁄₁₆″-dia.
entrance hole.*

NOTICE: If you live in a region or neighborhood where predation is a concern, incorporate a suitable predator guard into your plans. See pages 10 to 13.

Peterson-Style Bluebird House

While there are many different types of bluebird house designs, this nesting box is based on the popular and successful Peterson (or wedge) box that has been used quite successfully throughout the north-central and eastern United States. It features a triangular shape with a small floor that research seems to indicate bluebirds prefer. Because the oval entrance is slightly larger in overall area compared to a round entrance hole, be sure to incorporate predator guards to keep dangerous species at bay.

BUILDING THE BOX

1. Start by cutting all of your parts to size based on the cutting list and the illustration. To cut the bevels for the inner roof (B), floor (C), front (D), and back (E), simply set the blade on your jigsaw to the needed angle. (If you have access to a table saw, it will make cutting the beveled parts much quicker and easier.) Cut the front edge of the inner roof at 45°, the back edge of inner roof at 65°, the top edge of the front to 45°, the top edge of the back to 65°, and the back edge of the floor to 65°.

Drill a pair of 1⅜"-diameter holes to create an opening with the top 1" down from the top of the front panel and the bottom 2¼" down. Use a chisel to remove waste wood between the holes, forming an oval shape.

2. Use waterproof glue and 1⅝" exterior-rated screws to attach the left side to the back; then glue and screw the inner roof to the back and the left side. Attach the floor to the left side and the back, positioning it as shown in the illustration; then attach the right side to the house assembly.

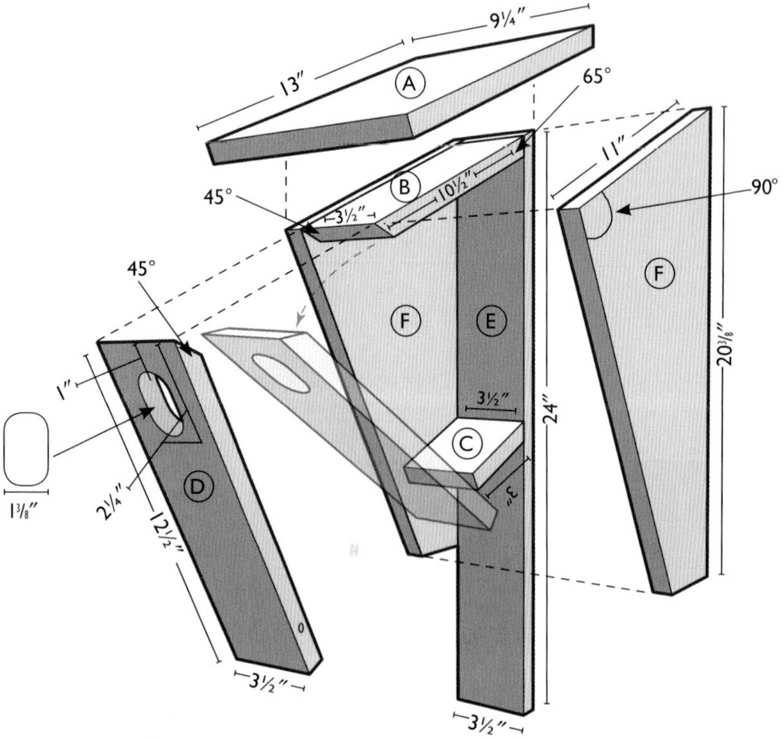

CUTTING LIST							
Key	Quan.	Part	Stock	Thickness	Width	Length	Comments
A	1	Outer roof	1×12	¾	9¼	13	
B	1	Inner roof	1×12	¾	3½	10¼	Cut ends at 45° & 65°
C	1	Floor	1×12	¾	3½	3	Cut one edge at 65°
D	1	Front	1×12	¾	3½	12½	Cut top edge at 45°
E	1	Back	1×12	¾	3½	24	Cut top edge at 45°
F	2	Sides*	1×12	¾	11	20⅜	

*Rough dimensions; see illustration for final dimensions

HARDWARE & SUPPLIES NEEDED		
1×12 × 6-ft. board (2)	2″ galvanized ring-shank nails	Waterproof wood glue
1⅝″ galvanized wood screws	Nail-in electrical cable tack	

Assemble the house using glue and 1⅝″ exterior wood screws driven into countersunk pilot holes.

3. Use glue and screws to attach the outer roof to the house, centering it on the inner roof. While the glue dries, drill the entrance hole in the front panel. Start by drilling a 1⅜″–wide hole 1″ below the top edge of the front panel (see illustration). Drill a second hole so that its bottom edge is 2¼″ down from the top edge of the hole you just drilled; then use a hammer and chisel to clean out the waste between the two holes.

4. Mount the front panel to the box assembly by driving 2″ ring-shank nails 2″ from the bottom edge of the sides through the sides and into the outer edges of the front piece—these nails will serve as hinges to open the box for cleaning and inspection. Lastly, attach nail-in electrical cable tacks as shown in the illustration to serve as latches that secure the front panel in place, and your bluebird house is ready to mount.

NOTICE: *If you live in a region or neighborhood where predation is a concern, incorporate a suitable predator guard into your plans. See pages 10 to 13.*

Flycatcher Nesting Box

There are at least thirty-six species of flycatchers in North America. The southern part of the continent, where the climate and the habitat is more to their liking, has the most species, but throughout most of the United States, the Great Crested and the Ash-throated Flycatchers are the most common.

Essentially a larger version of the Eastern Bluebird house, this design utilizes a flat roof and a larger 2″-dia. entrance hole. While it's primarily designed for the Great Crested Flycatcher, this nesting box can also be used by the Ash-throated Flycatcher of the western United States.

One of the more unusual habits of the Great Crested Flycatcher is its tendency to use shed snakeskins in its nest construction.

VITAL STATISTICS

GREAT CRESTED FLYCATCHER
(*Myiarchus crinitus*)

Size: 8.5″
Number of eggs: 4–8
Length of incubation: 13–15
Broods per season: 1
Food: insects, fruits, berries
Range: summer, eastern half of the continental United States; winter, migrates to the tropics

ABOUT THE BIRD

Flycatchers are somewhat of a mystery. Research is still evolving regarding these raucous birds. Although common in open woodlands, flycatchers are heard more than they are seen, and you'll not soon forget their loud *whee-eep* call.

Flycatchers like open deciduous forests and edges of clearings, and will also frequent old orchards, pastures, and even some urban areas (provided there are enough large trees).

Great Crested Flycatchers will often return to the same nest box year after year, and their nests are quite unique in that they incorporate shed snakeskins into their nests. At first, scientists thought that the birds were doing this as a means of scaring away potential predators. But as it turns out, it seems the birds simply like crinkly things, as they will also readily use old cellophane or other crinkly, shiny material in nest building.

HOUSE PLACEMENT

Because other species of birds such as starlings, tree swallows, bluebirds, and small woodpeckers may be attracted to this birdhouse, follow these tips to ensure that you attract a flycatcher:

- Mount the box at least 8 feet above the ground.

- Locate the box fairly close to woodlands.

- Orient the box so that the entrance hole faces a clear flight path.

- Place 1–2 inches of wood chips in the bottom of the box. (Do not use cedar wood chips.)

- As a mounting option, use a 3–4-foot length of chain or flexible cable to hang the box from an appropriate tree branch.

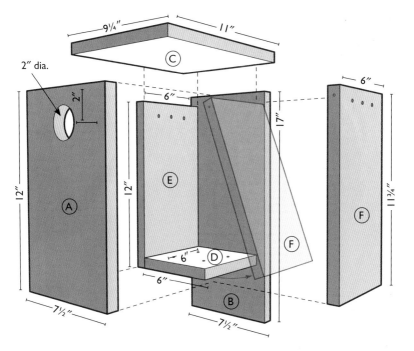

CUTTING LIST							
Key	Quan.	Part	Stock	Thickness	Width	Length	Comments
A	1	Front	1×10	¾	7½	12	Center a 2″ hole 2″ from top
B	1	Back	1×10	¾	7½	17	
C	1	Roof	1×10	¾	9¼	11	
D	1	Floor	1×10	¾	6	6	Drill four ¼″ holes for drainage
E	1	Side	1×10	¾	6	12	
F	1	Side	1×10	¾	6	11¾	

HARDWARE & SUPPLIES NEEDED		
1×10 × 6-ft. board	1⅝″ galvanized wood screws or 2″ galvanized ring-shank nails	Nail-in electrical cable tack Waterproof wood glue

Drill a 2"-dia. entrance hole centered 2" from the top edge of the front.

BUILDING THE BOX

1. Cut the parts to the sizes listed in the cutting list.

2. Drill a 2"-dia. entrance hole centered 2" down from the top of the front (A).

3. Drill four ¼" holes for drainage in the floor (D).

4. Use glue and exterior-rated 1⅝" screws to attach the long side (E) to the inside face of the front (A); then glue and screw the assembly to the back (B).

5. Position the shorter swing-out side (F) so that it is flush with the bottom of the front (A); then drive two 2" ring-shank nails, one on each side, to serve as pivot points near the top of the swing-out side (F).

6. Glue and screw the roof (C) in place; then insert and screw in place the floor (D).

7. Remove one nail from a nail-in electrical cable tack; then nail the cable tack to the side edge of the front near the bottom to serve as a latch that keeps the swing-out side closed.

Use 2" galvanized ring-shank nails as pivot points for the side that serves as a swing-out inspection panel.

NOTICE: If you live in a region or neighborhood where predation is a concern, incorporate a suitable predator guard into your plans. See pages 10 to 13.

Northern Flicker Nesting Box

Woodpeckers of all types have long interested me. Whether it's the antics of the small Downy Woodpeckers at my feeders in the winter or the thrill of spotting a Pileated Woodpecker deep in a forest, I'm always amazed and impressed by their industrious nature.

This nesting box is designed for the Northern Flicker, one of the larger woodpeckers in North America. This box is exceptionally easy to build. In fact, your biggest challenge will come from figuring out a way to mount the house high enough, as flickers prefer nest boxes that are approximately 10 to 20 feet off the ground.

Unlike its relatives, the Northern Flicker spends most of its time on the ground, searching for ants and other insects to eat.

VITAL STATISTICS
NORTHERN FLICKER (Colaptes auratus)

Size: 12–14″

Number of eggs: 5–8

Length of incubation: 11–14 days

Broods per season: 1

Food: insects, larvae, seeds, nuts, suet

Range: summer, north to Alaska; winter, south to Mexico; year-round, continental United States

ABOUT THE BIRD

The Northern Flicker is a large woodpecker, surpassed in size only by the Pileated Woodpecker and the Ivory-billed Woodpecker (if it truly still exists, as reports of its sightings in recent years remain unverified). It is a primary cavity nester, meaning it prefers to live in holes that it has excavated itself. But with continued loss of habitat, flickers are turning more and more to nest boxes.

While most woodpeckers are known for hammering on trees in search of insects, flickers most often feed on the ground. It has a long, sticky tongue that it uses to catch ants wherever it can find them.

There are several subspecies of flickers; the Yellow-shafted Flicker is more common in the eastern parts of the United States, the Red-shafted Flicker is usually found in western states, and the Gilded Flicker inhabits the deserts of the Southwest.

HOUSE PLACEMENT

Northern Flickers prefer semiopen country, and dead trees provide the perfect place for them to take up residence. Because flickers prefer to excavate their own homes, it's important to follow these tips for the best chance of success at attracting these colorful woodpeckers:

• Mount the box 6–20 feet above the ground—the higher, the better.

• Place the box in a generally sunny location.

• Orient the box so that it faces away from prevailing weather.

• Tightly pack the box with wood shavings so that the flicker can simulate excavation. (Do not use cedar shavings, as these can be harmful.)

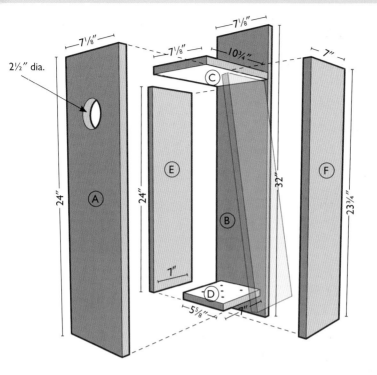

			CUTTING LIST			
Key	Quan.	Part	Stock	Thickness	Width	Length	Comments
A	1	Front	1×8	¾	7⅛	24	
B	1	Back	1×8	¾	7⅛	32	
C	1	Roof	1×8	¾	7⅛	10¾	
D	1	Floor	1×8	¾	5⅝	7	
E	1	Side	1×8	¾	7	24	
F	2	Side	1×8	¾	7	23¾	

HARDWARE & SUPPLIES NEEDED

1×10 × 6-ft. board

1⅝″ galvanized wood screws
2″ galvanized ring-shank nails

Nail-in electrical cable tack
Waterproof wood glue

After you've attached the long side to the back, use glue and screws to attach the front to the side.

BUILDING THE BOX

1. Cut all the parts to the sizes listed in the cutting list.

2. Use glue and 1⅝″ exterior-rated screws to attach the longer side (E) to the back (B); then attach the front (A) to the side (E).

3. Position the shorter swing-out side (F) so that it is flush with the bottom of the front (A); then drive two 2″ ring-shank nails, one on each side, to serve as pivot points near the top of the swing-out side (F).

4. Remove one nail from a nail-in electrical cable tack; then nail the cable tack to the side edge of the front near the bottom to serve as a latch that keeps the swing-out side closed.

5. Use a hole saw to cut a 2½″ entrance hole in the front (A) centered 19″ from the bottom edge.

6. Lastly, drill four ¼″ drainage holes in the floor (D) and glue and screw it in place; then attach the roof (C).

Because of the larger size of the entrance hole, you may find it easier to use a corded electric drill rather than a cordless model to bore the hole, as the corded drill has more torque and can handle the larger hole better.

NOTICE: If you live in a region or neighborhood where predation is a concern, incorporate a suitable predator guard into your plans. See pages 10 to 13.

Log-Style Woodpecker House

Perhaps because it so perfectly mimics a woodpecker's natural nesting preference—that of a cavity in a tree—I've had great success with this type of woodpecker house. It's not designed for any specific species, although Downy and Hairy Woodpeckers seem to be the most frequent users of this easy-to-build home.

You can use almost any large section of log for this house, provided it's at least 10″ in diameter and a minimum of 12″ tall. I've even used sections of old barn beams with just as much success.

The smallest woodpecker in North America, the Downy Woodpecker is found across most of the continent.

VITAL STATISTICS

DOWNY WOODPECKER
(*Picoides pubescens*)

Size: 7″
Number of eggs: 3–7
Length of incubation: 12 days
Broods per season: 1
Food: insects, larvae, seeds, nuts, berries, suet
Range: north to Alaska; south to Mexico; year-round, continental United States

ABOUT THE BIRD

With its black and white plumage and red patch on the back of its head, the Downy Woodpecker is easy to identify and closely resembles the slightly larger Hairy Woodpecker. It's a common visitor to backyard feeders, and it is fond of both sunflower seeds and suet.

Because of its diminutive size, the Downy Woodpecker is capable of eating insects that larger woodpeckers can't get to, such as those found in plant stems or larvae inside of plant galls.

Like other woodpeckers, the Downy Woodpecker does not sing. They do, however, emit loud chips that they can string together when excited. And contrary to common belief, the load, rapid drumming you hear is not a woodpecker attacking a tree in search of food; instead it is a woodpecker marking out territory or trying to attract a mate.

HOUSE PLACEMENT

Downy Woodpeckers prefer deciduous forests and areas with streams, and can also be found in old orchards, parks, and suburban environments. They have also been known to nest along fencerows and feed among tall weeds. For best results, follow these tips for log house placement:

- Mount the house 12–30 feet from the ground.

- If possible, chose a dead tree on which to mount the house.

- Line the bottom of the house with 2–3 inches of wood chips. (Do not use cedar wood chips.)

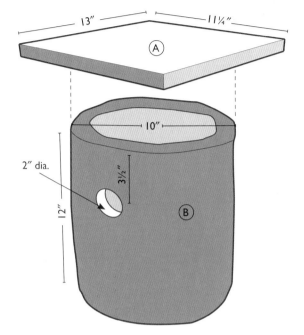

CUTTING LIST							
Key	Quan.	Part	Stock	Thickness	Width	Length	Comments
A	1	Roof	1×12	¾	11¼	13	
B	1	Body	Log		10″ dia.	12″ tall	

HARDWARE & SUPPLIES NEEDED		
10″-dia. log, roughly 12″ tall	1⅝″ galvanized wood screws	Waterproof wood glue

BUILDING THE BOX

1. Find a section of log that's at least 10″ in diameter and a minimum of 12″ in height. I removed the bark from the log for my house because it was already loose, but if it is still secure, feel free to leave it on.

2. Cut the roof (A) to the size shown in the cutting list.

3. Excavate the interior of the log. While there are many ways to do this, I used an electric drill and an auger bit to repeatedly drill into the body of the log and then removed the waste using a hammer and chisel. Just be sure to leave at least 1″ of thickness for the floor of the cavity.

4. Bore a 2″ entrance hole centered 3½″ from the top edge of the log.

5. Use glue and 1⅝″ exterior-rated screws to attach the roof (A) to the log.

Use an electric drill outfitted with an auger bit to excavate the interior of the log. Be careful as you drill, as an auger bit can aggressively twist the drill if the bit jams in the log while spinning.

Center the roof over the log and then use glue and exterior-rated screws to attach it in place on top of the log.

NOTICE: If you live in a region or neighborhood where predation is a concern, incorporate a suitable predator guard into your plans. See pages 10 to 13.

Wood Duck Nesting Box

The population of this colorful duck dropped so low in the 1930s that it was considered to be on the verge of extinction, all because of overhunting, logging, and the loss of forested wetlands. Today, however, the Wood Duck is one of the most common waterfowl, thanks to reforestation programs, the development of protected wetlands, increased hunting regulations, and the use of nesting boxes such as this one.

Except for its unusual oval-shaped hole and the scoring on the inside face of the front of the box that enables the little ducks to get out when they're ready to fledge, this box is easy to construct. It incorporates a swing-out side that's mounted on two heavy-duty brass hinges to make inspection and cleaning easier.

The exceptionally colorful Wood Duck is hard to miss, although they prefer more cover than most other species of ducks.

VITAL STATISTICS
WOOD DUCK (*Aix sponsa*)

Size: 18–20″
Number of eggs: 10–12
Length of incubation: 30 days
Broods per season: 1 or 2
Food: seeds, fruits, small aquatic or terrestrial animals
Range: summer, north to lower Canada; winter, south to Texas; year-round, Atlantic Coast west to the Mississippi River

ABOUT THE BIRD

Wood Ducks are secondary cavity nesters, meaning that they do not excavate their own holes as woodpeckers do. Instead, they search for abandoned holes or naturally occurring cavities in tree trunks.

Wood Ducks prefer more cover than most species of waterfowl and search out areas such as flooded open woodlands with small areas of open water. Small naturally occurring bodies of water and beaver ponds also make good wood duck environments.

Because Wood Ducks do not excavate their own holes, they rely on debris left behind by former residents of the hole or cavity, and it's not until the female has laid her eggs that she begins to add any material to the nest—plucked feathers from her own body.

After the eggs hatch, the young generally leave the nest within 24 hours by climbing to the entrance hole and jumping out, sometimes from incredible heights of over 100 feet! For that reason, it's important to include a way for the nestlings to successfully climb up to the hole—in this case a series of parallel gouges on the inside face of the front of the box.

HOUSE PLACEMENT

Wood Ducks prefer wetlands that combine flooded shrubs, water-tolerant trees, and small areas of open water, and they prefer to nest directly over or adjacent to water. For best results, follow these tips when choosing a site for your nesting box:

• Pick a location over or very close to water.

• Mount the house at least 4 feet above water, and 5½ feet above the ground.

• Mount the box high enough to avoid any potential floodwater.

• Install the box near nut- or berry-producing trees.

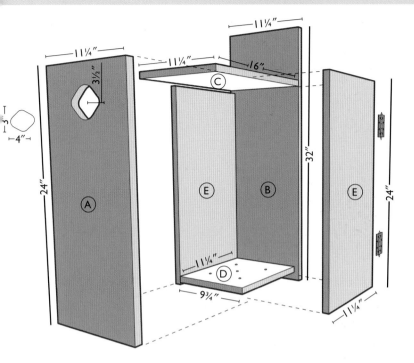

CUTTING LIST

Key	Quan.	Part	Stock	Thickness	Width	Length	Comments
A	1	Front	1×12	¾	11¼	24	
B	1	Back	1×12	¾	11¼	32	
C	1	Roof	1×12	¾	11¼	16	
D	1	Floor	1×12	¾	11¼	9¾	Drill four ¼″-dia. drainage holes
E	2	Sides	1×12	¾	11¼	24	

HARDWARE & SUPPLIES NEEDED

1×12 × 12-ft. board	1⅝″ galvanized wood screws 4″ brass hinges (2)	Waterproof wood glue

- Make sure that vegetation does not block the front of the box.

- Fill the box with 3–6 inches of wood chips or shavings. (Do not use cedar shavings.)

BUILDING THE BOX

1. Cut all the parts to size according to the sizes shown in the cutting list.

2. To create the oval-shaped entrance hole, start by drawing out the hole to the dimensions shown in the illustration. Make sure to center the hole 3½″ down from the top edge of the front (A). Drill a hole large enough for the blade of your jigsaw to penetrate along the penciled outline of the hole; then insert the jigsaw blade and cut the entrance hole along the penciled line.

3. Because the nestlings will need something to grab onto as they climb out of the house, use either a gouge or a rotary tool to score the inside face of the front (A) from the bottom of the entrance hole to just above the location of the floor.

The easiest way to drill the oval-shaped entrance hole is with a jigsaw. Simply drill a pilot hole that's big enough to allow the saw blade to penetrate the wood and then cut along the outline of the hole.

4. Use glue and 1⅝″ exterior-rated screws to attach one side (E) to the back (B); then glue and screw the front to the side.

5. Drill four ¼″-dia. drainage holes in the floor (D); then use glue and screws to attach the floor (D) and the roof (C) in place.

6. To allow for easy cleaning and inspection, use a pair of heavy-duty 4″ brass hinges to attach the remaining side (E) to the back (B). Drive a screw through the side and into the edge of the floor to secure the side in place. *Note:* While some wood duck houses have a smaller hatch for cleaning, I prefer to have the entire side open in case I need to repair the wire mesh egress ladder.

Because the little ducks need a way to climb out when they are ready to leave the nest, carve a series of parallel grooves on the inside face of the front of the house.

NOTICE: *If you live in a region or neighborhood where predation is a concern, incorporate a suitable predator guard into your plans. See pages 10 to 13.*

American Kestrel Nesting Box

I saw my first American Kestrel (also referred to as a Sparrow Hawk) when I was quite young, and at the time I thought it looked like a little brightly painted fighter plane. It's the smallest and most social hawk in North America, and like other insect-eating birds, the kestrel greatly suffered from the use of persistent pesticides such as DDT during the middle of the twentieth century. Thanks to aggressive nesting box campaigns, and tighter controls on pesticides, the kestrel has made a strong comeback.

Like the other square-design boxes in this book, this nesting box is easy to build—just make sure to mount it high enough so that a kestrel will want to use it.

The American Kestrel is the only cavity-nesting hawk in North America, and thanks to its brilliant plumage, it is easily recognizable.

VITAL STATISTICS
AMERICAN KESTREL (*Falco sparverius*)

Size: 9–12″

Number of eggs: 3–7

Length of incubation: 29–31 days

Broods per season: 1

Food: insects, frogs, bats, small reptiles, small birds

Range: summer, continental United States north to lower Alaska; winter, south to Panama; year-round in the temperate Midwest, including the Atlantic seaboard across to the Pacific coast.

ABOUT THE BIRD

A bird of the open country, the American Kestrel prefers meadows and grassy areas, abandoned fields, and other open environments. They can also be found in open wooded areas, deserts, and unforested mountainsides, and have even adapted to along highways and in some suburban situations.

They nest solely in cavities and rely on naturally occurring ones in dead trees or holes abandoned by other birds. When using a nesting box, they require a perch installed *inside* the box approximately 3 inches below the entrance hole for the nestlings' use.

HOUSE PLACEMENT

When looking for a house site, find a location that includes plenty of open land, preferably 1 acre or more, that provides plenty of hunting space. Follow these tips for the best chance of attracting an American Kestrel:

- Mount the box at least 10 feet above the ground, preferably 20–30 feet above the ground.

- Orient the box away from prevailing weather.

- Place the box near trees with dead limbs, telephone poles, or other structures where the bird can perch while hunting.

- To aid the nestlings in fledging, carve a series of parallel gouges on the inside face of the front of the box.

- Make sure there is a clear area in front of the house to allow for a flyway.

- Fill the box with 1–2 inches of wood chips or shavings. (Do not use cedar shavings.)

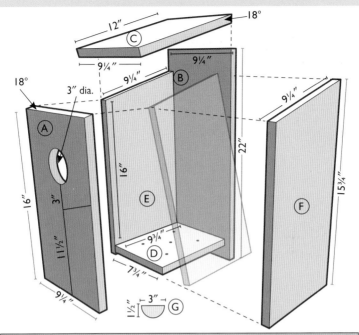

CUTTING LIST

Key	Quan.	Part	Stock	Thickness	Width	Length	Comments
A	1	Front*	1×10	¾	9¼	16	Bevel top edge at 18° angle
B	1	Back	1×10	¾	9¼	22	
C	1	Roof*	1×10	¾	9¼	12	Bevel rear edge at 18° angle
D	1	Floor	1×10	¾	9¼	7¾	Drill four ¼" holes for drainage
E	1	Side*	1×10	¾	9¼	16	Cut top end at 18° angle
F	2	Side*	1×10	¾	9¼	15¾	Cut top end at 18° angle
G	1	Perch	1×10	¾	1½"	3"	Cut from waste from entrance hole

*Rough dimensions; see illustration for final dimensions

HARDWARE & SUPPLIES NEEDED

1×10×8-ft. cedar board   2" galvanized ring-shank nails   Nail-in electrical cable tack
1⅝" galvanized wood screws   Waterproof wood glue

It's not necessary to use power tools to build birdhouses. A good quality handsaw will cut just as well as a jigsaw.

BUILDING THE BOX

1. Cut all the parts according to the sizes shown in the cutting list. Bevel the top edge of the front (A) and the back edge of the roof (C) at 18°.

2. Use a hole saw to drill a 3″-dia. entrance hole centered 11½″ from the bottom edge of the front (A).

3. Using the scrap from the entrance hole, create a semicircular perch (G) and then glue and screw it to the inside face of the front (A), positioning it 3″ below the bottom of the entrance hole.

4. Use a gouge or a rotary tool to carve a series of parallel grooves on the inside face of the front (A) running from just below the perch to just above the floor.

5. Use glue and 1⅝″ exterior-rated screws to attach the long side (E) to the back (B); then glue and screw the front (A) to the side (E).

6. Drill four ¼″-dia. drainage holes in the floor (D) and then glue and screw it in place.

Cut the circular waste from the entrance hole in half to make the perch; then glue and screw it to the inside face of the front 3″ down from the bottom edge of the entrance hole.

7. Position the shorter swing-out side (F) so that it is flush with the bottom of the front (A); then drive two 2″ ring-shank nails, one on each side, to serve as pivot points near the top of the swing-out side (F).

8. Remove one nail from a nail-in electrical cable tack; then nail the cable tack to the side edge of the front near the bottom to serve as a latch that keeps the swing-out side closed.

9. Glue and screw the roof to the assembly.

Barred Owl Nesting Box

Owls in general have long been associated with the mysterious and supernatural, and in fact they are extremely beneficial birds, feeding primarily on small rodents. I, myself, delight in spotting and attracting owls, and I consider myself quite fortunate to have had more than a few take up residence in the boxes I've built.

This nesting box features a large side-facing opening that, thanks to its size, makes it easy to clean and inspect the box. Just make sure to monitor it for squirrels, as they will readily take up residence in it.

The heavily streaked and spotted Barred Owl is one of only three species of large owls in North America that features dark eyes.

VITAL STATISTICS
BARRED OWL (*Strix varia*)

Size: 16–24″

Number of eggs: 2–4

Length of incubation: 23–32 days

Broods per season: 1

Food: mice and other small mammals, snakes and other small reptiles, frogs, bats, birds such as quail, grouse, doves, and other species of owls

Range: year-round, East Coast west to the Rockies and north into Lower Canada

ABOUT THE BIRD

The Barred Owl is a brown-gray owl with white spots on the back and white streaks on the belly and breast (from which it gets its name). It has no ear tufts, and its eyes are brown rather than the more common yellow.

Barred Owls live in heavy deciduous forests and have a tendency to prefer wetter locations such as wooded swamps or poorly drained forests. Some research seems to indicate that the wetter, the better, and that may relate not only to their diet of frogs, snakes, and other small reptiles and amphibians, but also to how undisturbed swampy areas tend to be compared to drier forests.

Barred Owls are very vocal. Its standard call is a series of hoots that sounds like someone saying, "*Who-cooks-for-you.*" It has a range of other calls, ranging from yelps to barks to monkey-like squalls, and it often will answer back when people mimic its call.

Barred Owls prefer to use existing tree cavities or holes made by other birds or animals. And they're early nesters—as early as January, these large owls start their nest-building activities.

One behavior that is unique to the Barred Owl is the young's ability to climb trees. By grasping the bark with their beaks and working their legs up the tree, they can climb back to their perch if they fall from the nest.

HOUSE PLACEMENT

Because Barred Owls will often prospect a potential nest site up to a year before actually moving in, it's important to be patient when trying to provide a home for these nocturnal birds. For the best chance of success, follow these tips:

• Mount the house at least 20 feet above the ground.

• Choose a site that is at least 200 feet from the nearest human residence.

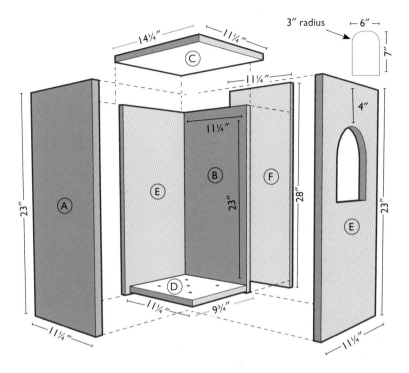

CUTTING LIST						
Key	Quan.	Part	Stock	Thickness	Width	Length	Comments
A	1	Front	1×12	¾	11¼	23	
B	1	Back	1×12	¾	11¼	23	
C	1	Roof	1×12	¾	11¼	14½	
D	1	Floor	1×12	¾	9¾	11¼	Drill four ¼″ holes for drainage
E	2	Sides	1×12	¾	11¼	23	
F	1	Mount	1×12	¾	11¼	28	

*Rough dimensions; see illustration for final dimensions

HARDWARE & SUPPLIES NEEDED		
1×12×12-ft. board	1⅝″ galvanized wood screws	Waterproof wood glue

After tracing the dimensions of the entrance hole onto one of the sides, use your jigsaw to cut out the arched hole.

- Because young owls need a place to perch once they fledge, choose a tree with branches close to the box.

- If possible, choose a site that has standing water within 200 feet of the nest site.

BUILDING THE BOX

1. Cut all the parts to the sizes shown in the cutting list.

2. Draw the entrance hole to the dimensions shown in the illustration on the outside face of one of the sides (E). Drill a hole to allow the blade of your jigsaw to penetrate the wood, and then using the jigsaw, cut the entrance hole.

3. Use glue and 1⅝″ exterior-rated screws to attach the sides (E) to the back (B).

4. To attach the mount (F), drive screws through the inside face of the back (B) and into the mount.

5. Glue and screw the front (A) to the sides (E).

6. Drill four ¼″ drainage hole through the floor (D); then glue and screw the floor and the roof (C) to the birdhouse assembly.

This house design is unique in that the entrance for it is on one of the sides rather than on the front.

NOTICE: *If you live in a region or neighborhood where predation is a concern, incorporate a suitable predator guard into your plans. See pages 10 to 13.*

Screech Owl Nesting Box

The first time I heard the call of the Screech Owl—which rarely sounds like an actual screech but more like a melancholy whistle—I was on a Cub Scout camp-out, and I have to admit it scared me. When I learned, however, of its diminutive size, I felt rather foolish, as the little owl is no bigger than the bird identification book I had in my backpack.

This box (used by both the Eastern and Western Screech Owl) is quite similar to the nesting box for the American Kestrel, except for a slightly smaller entrance hole and the elimination of the semicircular inside perch that the kestrel needs. Like many of the designs in this book, the box features a swing-out side for easy cleaning.

A permanent resident in its range, the Screech Owl is often the most common predator in wooded suburban and urban areas.

VITAL STATISTICS

EASTERN SCREECH OWL (*Otus asio*)

Size: 8–10″

Number of eggs: 2–8

Length of incubation: 26 days

Broods per season: 1

Food: small vertebrates and invertebrates, including insects, spiders, crayfish, small mammals, reptiles, amphibians, birds, and fish

Range: year-round, eastern and central United States, west to the Rockies

ABOUT THE BIRD

Screech Owls—both Eastern and Western—are solitary birds. They exist in two different color phases, red and gray, with the red being more common in the southern portion of its range. It has bright yellow eyes, a pale beak, and ear tufts that they can lower, giving their heads at times a rounded appearance.

After the eggs are laid, the male owl will feed the female, and will assist in feeding the young owlets. But as the chicks get older, both parents will withhold food outside the nest, thus encouraging the chicks to fledge.

HOUSE PLACEMENT

Screech Owls will inhabit most wooded landscapes, and they often prefer open woodland with little shrub cover, which helps in foraging and spotting potential predators. For the best chance of success in attracting Screech Owls to a nesting box, follow these tips:

- Mount the box 15–25 feet above the ground.

- Choose a straight-trunked tree that is wider than the box itself.

- Place about 1 inch of dried leaf debris in the bottom of the box.

- Place the box in a shady location.

- Orient the box so there is a clear flight path from the entrance hole.

- This is one of the few boxes that can be painted—choose a dark brown paint or stain, and apply it only to the outside.

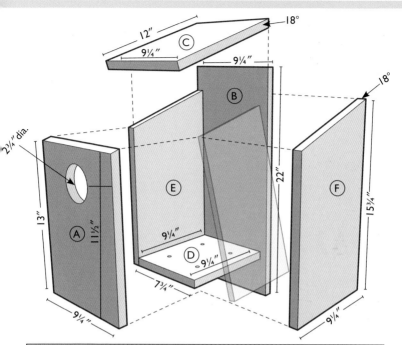

CUTTING LIST

Key	Quan.	Part	Stock	Thickness	Width	Length	Comments
A	1	Front*	1×10	¾	9¼	13	Bevel top edge at 18° angle
B	1	Back	1×10	¾	9¼	22	
C	1	Roof*	1×10	¾	9¼	12	Bevel rear edge at 18° angle
D	1	Floor	1×10	¾	9¼	7¾	Drill four ¼″ holes for drainage
E	1	Side*	1×10	¾	9¼	16	Cut top end at 18° angle
F	2	Side*	1×10	¾	9¼	15¾	Cut top end at 18° angle

*Rough dimensions; see illustration for final dimensions

HARDWARE & SUPPLIES NEEDED

1×10×8-ft. board
1⁵⁄₈″ galvanized wood screws

2″ galvanized ring-shank nails

Nail-in electrical cable tack
Waterproof wood glue

Use either a handsaw or a jigsaw and cut the top of the sides (E) at 18°.

BUILDING THE BOX

1. Cut all the parts according to the sizes shown in the cutting list. Bevel the top edge of the front (A) and the back edge of the roof (C) at 18°.

2. Use a hole saw to drill a 2¾″-dia. entrance hole centered 11½″ from the bottom edge of the front (A).

3. To provide an aid for the owlets to leave the box, use a gouge or a rotary tool to carve parallel grooves on the inside face of the front of the box running from just below the hole to just above the floor.

4. Use glue and 1⅝″ exterior-rated screws to attach the long side (E) to the back (B); then glue and screw the front (A) to the side (E).

5. Drill four ¼″-dia. drainage holes in the floor (D) and the glue and screw it in place.

6. Position the shorter swing-out side (F) so that it is flush with the bottom of the front (A); then drive two 2″ ring-shank nails, one on each side, to serve as pivot points near the top of the swing-out side (F).

7. Remove one nail from a nail-in electrical cable tack; then nail the cable tack to the side edge of the front near the bottom to serve as a latch that keeps the swing-out side closed.

8. Glue and screw the roof to the assembly.

Use a gouge or a rotary tool to carve a series of parallel grooves on the inside face of the front of the box.

Barn Owl Nesting Box

Perhaps the most unique-looking of all the owl species, the Barn Owl is easily identified by its heart-shaped face (sometimes referred to as a "monkey" face), and its gasping screech of a call can raise the hair on the back of the neck of even the most intrepid birder. Sadly, its numbers are in decline because of loss of habitat such as old barns and other dilapidated buildings where it likes to roost.

This nesting box is built from exterior-rated plywood and provides an ideal home for Barn Owls. It has a hinged end that allows for easy cleaning and inspection, and while I used brass screws and grommets for construction, any outdoor-rated screw will work.

With its white body, long legs, dark eyes, and heart-shaped face, the Barn Owl is easily identifiable.

VITAL STATISTICS
BARN OWL (*Tyto alba*)

Size: 14–20″
Number of eggs: 2–12
Length of incubation: 29–34 days
Broods per season: 1–3
Food: small mammals such as rodents and shrews
Range: year-round, southern half of the continental United States, west to Pacific Coast and east along the Atlantic seaboard

ABOUT THE BIRD

Barn Owls prefer open habitats such as grasslands, marshes, fields, and open woodlands with old buildings such as barns or abandoned outbuildings. Larger than the Screech Owl but smaller than the Great Horned Owl, they need large areas of open land where they can hunt for rodents, shrews, and other small birds.

Like many owls, the Barn Owl swallows its prey whole; they later cough up pellets of material they could not digest such as bones and hair. And while the Barn Owl has excellent night vision, it often hunts by sound alone. In fact, its ability to locate prey by sound alone is the highest of any animal that has ever been tested.

HOUSE PLACEMENT

Because of the Barn Owl's preference for abandoned or old buildings, one of the most successful tactics for attracting a nesting pair is to mount the house on or in an old barn. To have the greatest chance of success, follow these tips:

- Mount the box 20–25 feet above the ground.

- Choose a location where there is plenty of open hunting space.

- If mounting the box inside a structure, make sure there are adequate openings in the structure itself to allow the owl to come and go as needed.

- If there is not sufficient access, one option is to cut a hole through the structure's wall and attach the box directly behind the hole on the inside of the wall so that the hole feeds directly into the nest box.

- If mounting to the outside of an old structure, place the box up high in a protected location.

- Use strong mounting hardware to secure the box to the barn wall, as the combined weight of the owl and the box is quite heavy.

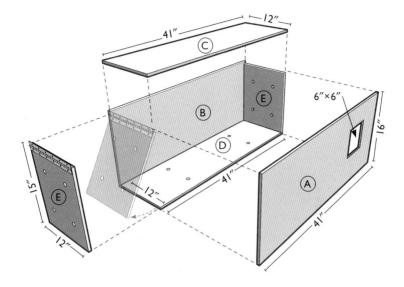

CUTTING LIST

Key	Quan.	Part	Stock	Thickness	Width	Length	Comments
A	1	Front	Ply	½	16	41	
B	1	Back	Ply	½	16	41	
C	1	Top	Ply	½	12	41	
D	1	Bottom	Ply	½	12	41	Drill four ¾″ drainage holes
E	1	Ends	Ply	½	12	15	Drill four ¾″ ventilation holes

HARDWARE & SUPPLIES NEEDED

4×8×½″ exterior-rated plywood sheet	1⅝″ galvanized or brass wood screws	1½″ × 12″ piano hinge Waterproof wood glue

BUILDING THE BOX

1. Cut all the parts to size from ½″-thick exterior-rated plywood as shown in the cutting list.

2. To cut the 6″ × 6″ square entrance hole, first trace its outline onto the front panel (A). Drill a pilot hole large enough to allow the blade of your jigsaw to penetrate the plywood, and then cut along the traced outline of the opening.

3. Drill four ¾″ drainage holes in the bottom (D). Use glue and 1⅝″ exterior-rated screws to attach the top (C) and the bottom (D) to the back (B); then glue and screw the front (A) to the assembly.

4. Drill four ¾″ ventilation holes in both of the end panels (E). Glue and screw the end panel that's closest to the entrance hole in place.

5. Use a 1½″ × 12″ piano hinge to attach the remaining end panel (E). Screw the hinge first to the top (C) and then attach the end panel to the hinge. To keep the panel from accidentally opening, drive a screw through the bottom (D) and into the end panel (E).

Use your jigsaw to cut the square entrance hole in the front panel.

I used brass wood screws and grommets for a decorative look, but any exterior-rated screw will work just as well.

Basic Platform Feeder

Sunflower seed—especially black oil sunflower seed—is one of the best type of bird feed you can offer your feathered friends. When compared to striped sunflower seeds, black oil seeds are meatier and have a higher oil content, giving birds more nutrition and calories in every bite. Black oil seeds also have thinner shells, making them easier for small birds to crack.

One of the easiest types of bird feeders you can build is a simple platform to hold sunflower seed. Consisting of nothing more than a few pieces of wood, it's a modification of one that I've been building for years. It's open design attracts many different species of seed-eating birds, but keep an eye out for squirrels, as they are voracious eaters and will happily camp out on the feeder and stuff themselves until all the seed is gone.

BUILDING THE BOX

1. Cut all the parts according to the sizes shown in the cutting list. Miter the ends of the sides (D) and the ends (E) at 45°.

2. Use glue and 1⅝″ exterior-rated screws to attach the sides (D) and the ends (E) to the tray (C).

3. Attach the mount (B) to the back (A) by driving screws through the back and into the mount.

4. Glue and screw the tray assembly onto the mount as shown in the drawing.

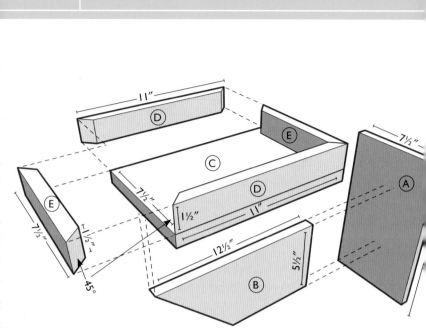

CUTTING LIST						
Key	Quan.	Part	Stock	Thickness	Width	Length	Comments
A	1	Back	1×8	¾	7½	13	
B	1	Mount	1×8	¾	5½	12½	
C	1	Tray	1×8	¾	7½	11	
D	2	Sides	1×2	¾	1½	11	Miter the ends at 45°
E	2	Ends	1×2	¾	1½	7½	Miter the ends at 45°

HARDWARE & SUPPLIES NEEDED

1×8 × 4-ft. board	1×2 × 4-ft. board	Waterproof wood glue
	1⅝″ galvanized wood screws	

While I mitered the sides and ends, you could choose a more simple construction by using butt joints instead of miters.

Basic Bin Feeder

Of all the types of seeds that are popular for wildlife feeding, sunflower seeds are by far the most popular. Species of birds that love sunflower seed include cardinals, titmice, mourning doves, juncos, grosbeaks, grackles, finches, pine siskins, jays, chickadees, nuthatches, and many other types of woodpeckers.

This feeder design is the natural evolution of the platform feeder. While it has a walled tray like the previous feeder, it also has a hinged bin that holds more seed and keeps it protected both from the elements and from squirrels.

BUILDING THE BOX

1. Start by cutting the parts to the sizes shown in the cutting list. Miter the ends of the end rails (B) and the side rails (C) to 45°.

2. Use glue and 1⅝" exterior-rated screws to attach the end rails and side rails to the tray (A).

3. Glue and screw the bin front (D) and the bin back (E) between the bin sides (F). Make sure that the top edges of all four parts are flush with each other.

4. Place the bin on top of the shelf between the side rails and against the back rail. To hold the bin in place, from underneath drive screws through the tray and into the ends of the bin sides.

MOUNTING FEEDERS

Many of the feeders in this book are designed to be mounted on poles or posts. One of the easiest ways I've found to mount feeders is by using threaded black pipe. Available at most home improvement and hardware stores, black pipe is available in many different diameters—I prefer 2"-dia. pipe. Stores will often cut the pipe to length for you and thread the end. (As a rule, purchase pipe 2 feet longer than the height at which you want your feeder so that you have ample length to drive into the ground.) All you then have to do is buy a threaded cap or a threaded flange for the pipe and screw it to the underside of the feeder. Drive the pipe into the ground where you want to install your feeder and thread the feeder onto the pipe.

5. Attach one 1″ brass hinges along the top edge of the bin back; then attach the hinges to the underside of the bin lid.

6. Lastly, install the brass screw-in hook and eye that will keep the top closed.

A screw-in brass hook and eye will keep the lid of the seed bin closed and protect its contents from both the elements and from foraging squirrels.

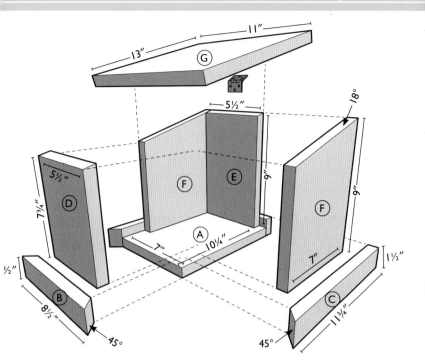

CUTTING LIST						
Key	Quan.	Part	Stock	Thickness	Width	Length	Comments
A	1	Tray	1×10	¾	7	10¼	
B	2	End rails	1×2	¾	1½	8½	Miter ends at 45°
C	2	Side rails	1×2	¾	1½	11¾	Miter ends at 45°
D	1	Bin Front	1×10	¾	5½	7¾	
E	1	Bin Back	1×10	¾	5½	9	
F	2	Bin Sides	1×10	¾	7	9	
G	1	Bin Lid	1×12	¾	11	13	

HARDWARE & SUPPLIES NEEDED

1×12 × 3-ft. board	1⅝" galvanized wood screws	Brass screw-in hook and eye
1×10 × 6-ft. board	1" brass hinges (1)	Waterproof wood glue
1×2 × 4-ft. board		

Finch Feeder

This feeder is built from common screw-together PVC plumbing components available at most home improvement or hardware stores, and it's designed to hold niger seed. Although commonly called thistle seed, niger seed is imported primarily from India, Ethiopia, Nepal, and Burma. It typically will not germinate under your feeders, as the USDA requires that all niger seed imported to this country be heat-treated to sterilize the seed (meaning that you don't need to worry about growing weeds from spilled seed).

Niger seed is a favorite food for a wide variety of finches, siskins, redpolls, and other small-billed seed-eating birds. The seed can quickly dry out and lose its nutritional oil, so throw away any uneaten seed regularly. And make sure to not let the seed get wet or moldy in the feeder, as it then can become harmful for birds.

BUILDING THE FEEDER

1. Drill eight ⅜"-dia. feeding holes and eight ¼"-dia. perch holes through a 24"-long section of Schedule 40 PVC pipe. You'll drill the holes in pairs, as they are positioned directly across from each other. Locate the holes as you like; just keep the drill perpendicular to the pipe as you work.

2. Use a hacksaw to cut to length four ¼"-dia. × 8"-long steel rod perches.

3. Push a 2"-dia. end cap onto the bottom of the PVC pipe; then use ¾" hex-head self-tapping screws to secure the end cap to the pipe.

4. Push a 2"-dia. threaded PVC coupler onto the top of the PVC pipe and secure it in place with two ¾" hex-head self-tapping screws.

5. Insert the steel perches into the perch holes on one side of the pipe and out the corresponding holes on the other side. Use a small dab of epoxy to secure the perches in place.

6. Install a threaded hook at the top center of the 2"-dia. threaded PVC cap. Fill the feeder with seed, screw the cap onto the pipe, and hang the feeder from a shepherd's hook or other appropriate hanger.

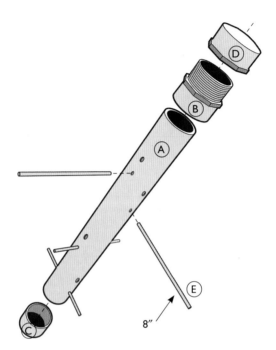

8″

CUTTING LIST

Key	Quan.	Part
A	1	2″ × 24″ Schedule 40 PVC tube for the body
B	1	2″ PVC threaded coupler
C	1	2″ PVC end cap
D	1	2″ PVC threaded cap
E	4	¼″-dia. × 8″ steel rod perches

HARDWARE & SUPPLIES NEEDED

2″-dia. × 24″ Schedule 40 PVC tube

¼″-dia. × 36″ steel rod

2″-dia. Schedule 40 PVC threaded coupler, end cap, and threaded cap

¾″ self-tapping hex head screws

Threaded hook

All the parts for the body of this feeder are made from common PVC plumbing parts that you can find at most hardware or home improvement stores.

Suet Feeder

Suet is another great food for attracting a wide variety of birds. In its natural form, suet is simply hard, raw beef fat and is available from local butchers or meat markets. For birding, however, suet is often blended and mixed with oats, seed, raisins, nuts, and other ingredients and then pressed into cakes.

This feeder is simple to build and is large enough to hold either a pressed suet cake or raw suet. It features a hinged top and a wire mesh front that gives birds plenty of access to the food inside.

BUILDING THE BOX

1. Cut all the parts according to the sizes shown in the cutting list. The sizes of the mount and the spacer block are not critical, so feel free to use existing scrap lengths if it is more convenient.

2. Use glue and 1⅝″ exterior-rated screws to attach the bottom (F) to the face of the back (C), flush with the bottom edge of the back.

3. Glue and screw the sides (D) to the back and bottom.

4. Attach a small 1″ brass hinge centered along the top edge of the back; then attach the top (E) to the hinge. Position the top so that its back edge is flush with the back edge of the back (C).

5. Glue and screw the spacer (B) to the center of the back (C) as shown in the drawing; then attach the mount (A) by driving screws though it and into the spacer.

6. Cut a 7¼″ × 9″ piece of ½″ galvanized wire mesh. Place it on the front of the feeder, lay the two cleats (G) on top of the mesh, aligned with the edges of the sides (D), and then fasten the cleats to the sides using 2″ galvanized ring-shank nails, thus trapping the mesh between the sides and the cleats.

Wood cleats that are nailed to the front edges of the sides hold the galvanized wire mesh in place.

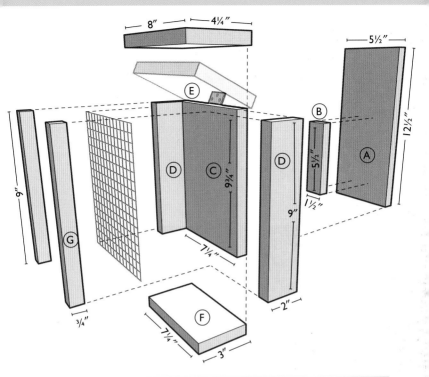

CUTTING LIST

Key	Quan.	Part	Stock	Thickness	Width	Length	Comments
A	1	Mount	1×8	¾	5½	12½	
B	1	Spacer	1×2	¾	1½	5½	
C	1	Back	1×8	¾	7¼	9¾	
D	2	Sides	1×8	¾	2	9	
E	1	Top	1×8	¾	4¼	8	
F	1	Bottom	1×8	¾	3	7¼	
G	2	Cleats	1×2	¾	¾	9	

HARDWARE & SUPPLIES NEEDED

1×8 × 4-ft. board

1×2 × 3-ft. board

1⅝" galvanized wood screws

2" galvanized ring-shank nails

1" brass hinge

7¼" × 9" piece of ½" wire mesh

Waterproof wood glue

Squirrel-Proof Feeder

One of the biggest problems you'll encounter with feeding wild birds is squirrels. These brazen, voracious eaters will consume every scrap of seed they can get their paws on. Not only will they drive your birdseed budget through the roof, but they will chase away the very birds that you hope to attract.

While there are many ready-to-install feeders that claim to be squirrel-proof, I have yet to find one that lives up to its promises. The sad fact is that squirrels are clever enough to get around most deterrents, and the best you can hope for is a compromise that makes it as difficult as possible for the squirrel to eat the seed but also provides easy access for birds to get to the seed.

This design is one I've been tweaking for a few years now. The steel rods that form the guard at the front are spaced close enough to prevent most squirrels from reaching the seed, while the spacing between the rods is large enough to allow birds access to the food.

BUILDING THE BOX

1. Cut all the wood parts to the sizes shown in the cutting list. Bevel the top edge of the back (B) and the front edge of the roof (D) to 18°.

2. Use glue and 1⅝″ exterior-rated screws to attach the sides (C) to the floor (A), aligning the sides so that they are flush with the bottom face of the floor.

3. Glue and screw the back (B) to the feeder assembly.

Sections of steel rods form a barrier that prevents squirrels from reaching most of the seed in this feeder, yet provides enough space for birds to have access to it.

4. Glue and screw the inner walls (F) to the inside faces of the sides (C), positioning them so that they are flush against the back (B).

5. Use a knife or a jigsaw outfitted with a fine-tooth blade to cut the clear polycarbonate to the size shown in the cutting list; then drill pilot holes and use 1″ trim head screws to attach it to the front edges of the inner walls (F). Position the polycarbonate so that it is flush with the top edge of the inner walls.

6. Glue and screw the front edge to the floor; then glue and screw the roof to the feeder assembly, aligning the roof so that it is flush with the front edges of the sides.

7. Set the lid in place; then use two 1″ brass hinges to attach the lid to the roof.

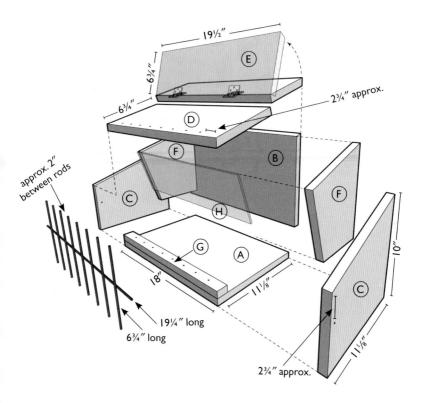

8. Use a hacksaw to cut the ⅛″-dia. steel rods into eight 6¾″-long lengths and one 19¼″-long section. Drill eight ⅛″-dia. holes through the roof, positioned according to the locations shown in the drawing, and drill one ⅛″-dia. hole through the left side, positioned as shown in the drawing.

9. Insert the shorter sections of the steel rod into the holes in the roof. Use a hammer to tap them into the top of the front edge (G) until they are flush with the top face of the roof; then use a few drops of cyanoacrylate glue (such as Crazy Glue) to secure them in place.

10. Insert the longer horizontal rod through the hole in the side. Tap and glue it into position as you did the vertical rods.

CUTTING LIST

Key	Quan.	Part	Stock	Thickness	Width	Length	Comments
A	1	Floor	1×12	¾	11⅛	18	
B	1	Back	1×12	¾	10¼	19½	Bevel top edge to 18°
C	2	Sides*	1×12	¾	11⅛	10	
D	1	Roof	1×8	¾	6¾	19½	Bevel front edge to 18°
E	1	Lid	1×8	¾	6¾	19½	
F	2	Inner walls*	1×12	¾	8	9¼	
G	1	Front edge	1×2	¾	1½	18	
H	1	Front	.093		5¾	18	Cut from 12×24 sheet of .093 Lexan

HARDWARE & SUPPLIES NEEDED

1×12 × 6-ft. board (1)
1×8 × 4-ft. board (1)
1×2 × 2-ft. board (1)
12″ × 24″ sheet of .093-thick clear polycarbonate (1)

⅛″-dia. × 48″ steel rod (3)
1″ brass hinges (2)
Brass hook and eye (1)

1⅝″ galvanized wood screws
Waterproof wood glue
Cyanoacrylate glue (such as Crazy Glue)

Deck Rail/Windowsill Feeder

A great way to enjoy bird watching is to set up a feeding station that's close to windows or glass doors. This seed feeder is designed to do just that and will either sit atop a deck railing or mount to brackets in front of a windowsill.

To mount the feeder to a deck railing, measure the width of the railing and then install two short lengths of 2 × 4 braces spaced to that measurement to the bottom of the feeder; then slip the feeder over the railing and drive a few screws either through the seed tray or through the 2 × 4 braces and into the railing beneath to secure it.

To mount the feeder against the wall of your house so that it sits at window height, first locate the studs in the exterior wall below the window where you want the feeder to reside. Screw two metal or wood shelf brackets to the house wall, making sure that the screws penetrate the studs; then screw the feeder to the shelf brackets.

BUILDING THE BOX

1. Cut all the parts to the sizes shown in the cutting list.

2. Use glue and 1⅝" exterior-rated screws to attach the seed bin front and back panels (B) to the seed bin side panels (C). Align all four parts so that their tops are flush.

3. Glue and screw the side rails (E) and the end rails (F) to the tray (D).

4. Attach a 1" brass hinge centered along the top of the seed bin's back panel (B); then align the lid (A) so that it sits squarely over the seed bin and attach the hinge to the lid.

5. Set the assembled seed bin over the tray. Make sure that it is centered and then screw it to the tray's side rails (E).

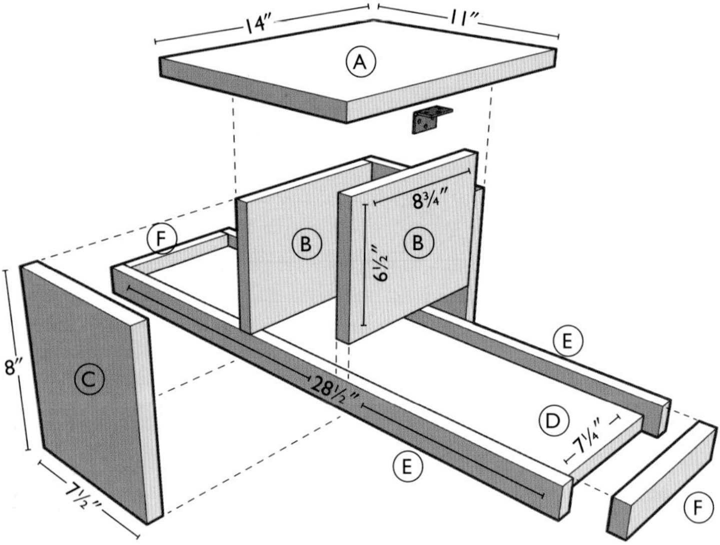

CUTTING LIST							
Key	Quan.	Part	Stock	Thickness	Width	Length	Comments
A	1	Lid	1×12	¾	11	14	
B	2	Front/Back	1×8	¾	6½	8¾	
C	2	Sides	1×8	¾	7½	8	
D	1	Tray	1×8	¾	7¼	27	
E	2	Side rails	1×2	¾	1½	28½	
F	2	End rails	1×2	¾	1½	7¼	

HARDWARE & SUPPLIES NEEDED		
1×12 × 2-ft. board	1×2 × 8-ft. board	1" brass hinge
1×8 × 6-ft. board	1⅝" galvanized wood screws	Waterproof wood glue

A weather-resistant brass hinge allows the lid to open and provides for easy filling of the seed bin.

Metal Canopy Feeder

Bird feeders do not need to be fancy, and in fact you can often build them from material you may have sitting around from past home improvement projects.

This feeder is a great example if repurposing old material. It's made from a few spare bits of cedar from other birdhouse projects and some extra aluminum flashing I had lying around from a roof repair I had done a few years back. It's a great variation to using wood, and the hex-head self-tapping screws give it a unique industrial look.

BUILDING THE BOX

1. Start by cutting all the parts to the sizes shown in the cutting list. Use a metal snips to cut the flashing to length.

2. Use glue and 1⅝" exterior-rated screws to attach the ends (B) and the sides (C) to the tray (A).

3. Use 1" galvanized hex-head self-tapping screws to attach the metal roof to the sides. For best results, double up the screws and drive them in pairs, one above the other.

4. To mount this feeder, either install it at the top of a wood post or use threaded black pipe driven into the ground and a threaded flange as I described earlier.

Use self-tapping hex-head screws to attach the roof (which is cut from aluminum flashing that's sold in rolls) to the sides.

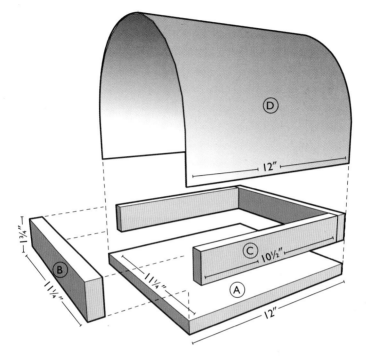

CUTTING LIST

Key	Quan.	Part	Stock	Thickness	Width	Length	Comments
A	1	Tray	1×12	¾	11¼	12	
B	2	Ends	1×2	¾	1¾	11¼	
C	2	Sides	1×2	¾	1¾	10½	
D	1	Roof			12	28	

HARDWARE & SUPPLIES NEEDED

1×12 × 3-ft. board
1×2 × 4-ft. board

12"-wide × 3-ft. roll of
aluminum flashing
1⅝" galvanized wood screws

1" galvanized hex-head
screws (16)
Waterproof wood glue

Peanut Butter Log Feeder

Keeping with the theme of using material that you already have on end, the versatile log feeder is perhaps the simplest of all feeders to build. It's been around for decades and is often used in children's craft classes as an entry-level project for young hands. There's no rhyme or reason to the placement of the holes—simply drill them where you think they will look the best based on the shape of your log.

Made from nothing more than a log and a few wood dowels to serve as perches, this feeder serves up a mixture of peanut butter, seeds, and dried fruit bits. To make the mixture, simply combine peanut better, sunflower seed, and dried fruit such as raisins in a bowl. Mix together and then pack it tightly into the holes in the feeder. Refrigerate any extra mix so that you always have more on hand to fill the feeder as the birds deplete it.

BUILDING THE BOX

1. Start by finding a log that looks attractive to you. Any species of wood will work, but try to find a log that's at least 18″ in length and 4–6″ in diameter.

2. Drill 2″-dia. holes 2–3″ deep to hold the peanut butter mixture. The placement of the holes is completely up to you, and you can even make the holes bigger or deeper if you'd like (depending on the size of log you're using).

3. Drill ¼″-dia. holes for the perches just below the holes for the peanut butter.

4. Cut a ¼″-dia. wood dowel into 3″-long sections; then apply glue to the perch holes and insert the dowels into the holes.

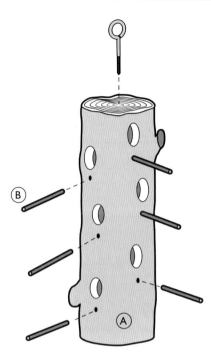

CUTTING LIST

Key	Quan.	Part
A	1	18–20″-long log, 4-6″ in diameter
B	12*	¼″-dia. × 3″ dowels

*While I used 12 dowels/feeding stations, drill as many as you think appropriate for your log.

HARDWARE & SUPPLIES NEEDED

Log that's visually appealing	1½″-dia. drill bit	1½″ screw eye
¼″-dia. wood dowel (length based on how many feeding stations you drill)	¼″-dia. drill bit	Waterproof wood glue

There's no formula for where to drill the holes for the peanut butter. Choose spots based on the shape of the log you're using and insert perches just below each feeding station.

Oriole Feeder

Orioles are beautiful birds, and by providing the right type of food for them, you can enjoy these colorful creatures throughout the summer. Orioles love sweet things, especially fruits, jelly, and nectar, and I've had great success over the years by offering them orange halves.

This feeder, which holds two orange halves, is very easy to build. Two nails serve as spikes on which I can impale the fruit, and by installing chain or flexible cable at each end, it's easy to hang this feeder from almost anywhere.

BUILDING THE BOX

1. Start by cutting the parts to the sizes shown in the cutting list. Use a jigsaw to cut the curved sides (B).

2. Drive two 2¼″ nails through the base (A) to serve as spikes on which to mount orange halves. Install.

3. To increase the feeder's visual appeal, paint it bright orange. Remember to use a nontoxic paint.

4. Install eye screws at the top of each side; then use chain or flexible cable to hang the feeder from a shepherd's hook or other convenient point.

ORIOLE FEEDING TIPS

- Avoid spraying pesticides that will remove the insects these birds eat. Depending on the oriole species, insects may make up to 90 percent of their diet, particularly during nesting season when young birds require more protein for healthy growth and development.

- Install the feeder near fruit-bearing shrubs and bushes.

- Plant a variety of nectar-producing flowers near the feeder to give orioles another natural food source.

- Do not offer fortified orange juice or orange-flavored drinks in place of oriole nectar.

- Keep nectar, fruit, and jelly feeders fresh by replacing the contents every few days and washing the feeders when necessary. In the hottest weather, feeders may need to be cleaned daily.

After tracing the outlines, use a jigsaw to cut the curved side panels of the feeder.

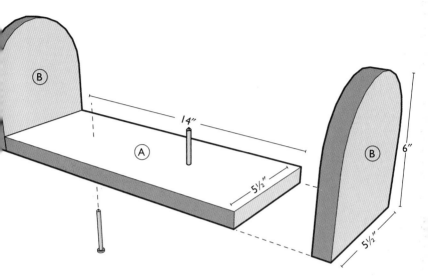

CUTTING LIST

Key	Quan.	Part	Stock	Thickness	Width	Length	Comments
A	1	Base	1×6	¾	5½	14	
B	2	Sides	1×6	¾	5½	6	

HARDWARE & SUPPLIES NEEDED

1×6 × 3-ft. board
1⅝" galvanized wood screws (4)

2¼" nails (2)
Eye screws (2)

Chain or flexible cable (to hang the feeder)
Waterproof wood glue

Seed Catcher

Because many seed feeders can create quite a mess, a seed catcher installed below your feeder can greatly help in keeping discarded seed hulls out of your lawn. Simple and easy to build, a seed catcher consists of nothing more than a square wood frame that has a section of window screening stapled to it. Install a hook to the bottom of an existing feeder from which you can hang the seed catcher, and then use lengths of chain or flexible cable to hang the catcher from the hook.

BUILDING THE BOX

1. Cut four lengths of what's commonly referred to as L molding to the length indicated in the cutting list. Miter the ends at 45°.

2. To build the frame, use 2″ × ½″-wide L brackets to join the four frame sections (A) together. If the tips of the screws poke through the underside of the wood molding, use a rotary tool or a file to trim them.

3. Cut a 19½″-square section of window screen material and staple it to the inside of the molding.

4. Install eye screws at each corner of the frame; then use chain or flexible cable to hang the seed catcher below your feeder.

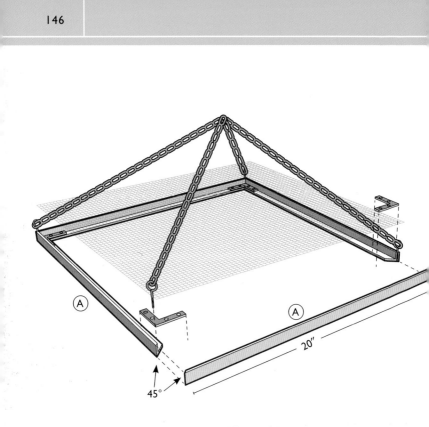

CUTTING LIST			
Key	Quan.	Part	Stock
A	4	Frame	20″-long sections of ⅝″ or ¾″ L molding

HARDWARE & SUPPLIES NEEDED

8-ft.-length of ⅝″ or ¾″ oak L molding

2″ × ½″ L brackets and screws (4)

19½″ square section of fine-mesh window screening

⅜″ T-50 weather-resistant staples

½″ screw eyes (4)

6 ft. of chain or flexible cable

Waterproof wood glue

After stapling the screen material in place, use a utility knife to cut away any excess material.

Serving Bowl Birdbath

When it comes to bathing, birds are not particular. As long as the water basin has enough depth for the birds to splash about in and has enough texture for their little feet to grab, they will be happy.

While there are many ready-to-use birdbaths available for purchase, some of the most attractive and unique come from items that you have lying about the house. Old pie tins, serving bowls, trays, or shallow planting trays can make excellent birdbaths, and you're saving money by repurposing something that you already own.

TIPS FOR BUILDING BIRDBATHS

- Build a birdbath that's shallow rather than deep, with no more than 3" of water at the bottom.

- Pick a water basin that has a graduated edge so that birds can ease their way into the water.

- Avoid an overly slick surface for the bowl so that birds do not feel as if they are going to slip into the water.

- If you use metal or glass, look for a bowl that has texture that a bird's feet can grab onto.

- If possible, add a small pump to your birdbath design to keep the water moving. Not only will the birds like it more, it will keep the water cleaner and cut down on mosquitoes.

This particular birdbath was made from nothing more than a spare textured-plastic shallow serving bowl, an extra flowerpot tray, and a old, tall glazed square planter that I had sitting around. I used silicone caulk to adhere all of the components together, and I regularly have birds waiting for their turn to bathe.

Be daring in your design. Use components that you would not normally think of for a bird bath, and do not be afraid to paint it in bright colors or in tones that match your garden.

Bejeweled Birdbath

This birdbath is an extension of being creative. It consists of a short, decorative pillar on which I used to set a plant and a flowerpot tray that I sealed with clear acrylic; I then used clear silicone caulk to adhere various colors of glass beads (which you can find at most craft stores) to the tray's surface. The pebbled surface that was the result provides enough traction for bathing birds, and the splash of color the birdbath creates is a great addition to my garden.

When building a birdbath of this nature, be bold. There are many different styles of ornamental glass beads available at craft stores, and there's no rule as to what you can or can't use. The garden in which I placed this birdbath has a lot of early-blooming lavender and salvia, as well as late-blooming hydrangea, which is why I opted for the red, white, and blue beads. But again, pick what works with your plants and fits your taste.

BIRDBATH POSITIONING TIPS

- Do not place a birdbath near areas where cats or other predators can hide. It's important that birds do not feel threatened when they are bathing.

- Place your birdbath within an easy flight path of low-hanging branches—that way, in the event that a predator does show up, birds can easily escape.

- Place your birdbath near your own house so that it is easy to fill and clean.

- If possible, position the birdbath near a window or glass door so that you can get the most enjoyment possible from watching the birds use it.

Concrete Birdbath

Many commercially made birdbaths are fashioned from concrete. Why? Because it's an inexpensive, strong, and durable material that's easy to work with. But while store-bought concrete birdbaths can be expensive, you can easily (and inexpensively) make your own.

This birdbath was made in one evening. I built a form for it from melamine boards (the same material that the white-faced shelving you find in home improvement stores is made from). You'll need a 40-lb. bag of concrete and chicken wire.

CARING FOR CONCRETE BIRDBATHS

- Concrete is a porous material and it can be hard to keep clean. On a regular basis, use a stiff brush to scrub the "pores" of the concrete surface to remove any algae or bacteria that might accumulate.

- Regularly fill the birdbath with clean, fresh water and remove any debris such as bird feathers, leaves, or seeds from the birdbath on a daily basis.

- Drain your birdbath before the first chance of a freeze, and don't be too eager to put it out in the early spring if the chance of a freeze still exists—ice can easily split a birdbath basin.

1. Cut the melamine to form the shapes of a square basin and a square pedestal; then screw it together. Do not use any glue, as you'll be disassembling the form after the concrete dries.

2. Spray the inside of the form with nonstick cooking spray—even though the melamine is naturally slick, the cooking spray will help the form release from the concrete even easier after the concrete is dry.

3. Mix the concrete according to the instructions on the bag—I like to keep my mix a little on the thick, stiff side, and I add a little dry colored powder to the mix (available where you buy the concrete)—and then begin packing it into the form. After you have an inch or so of concrete laid down, cut a square of chicken wire slightly smaller than the basin and embed it in the wet concrete.

4. Continue packing in the concrete, molding the indentation for the water basin as you work. (If you prefer, you can build a second smaller form and set it into the larger one, resting on top of the packed concrete, to block out the area for the water basin. Similarly, fill the mold for the basin with wet concrete and embed lengths of chicken wire into it as you work. After the concrete has cured for at least a day, disassemble the molds and remove the melamine boards.

Stone Birdbath

Just as with materials such as porcelain, terracotta, or glass, be creative with stone, concrete, and other building materials for your birdbath projects.

This birdbath, built primarily of small sections of polished stone that were mortared together, belongs to a good friend of mine and has been serving the feathered community for close to fifty years. His father originally built it to reside in a garden at his childhood home. But when the family moved, they took the birdbath with them and erected it at their new residence.

If you'd like to build something similar, start by talking with your local stone providers. Businesses such as cemetery monument crafters, stone countertop suppliers, and granite quarries often have small, broken bits of polished stone that they cannot use for any purpose, and these pieces often end up in a scrap pile. These pieces are inexpensive—even free sometimes—and for a small fee they will often polish them for you.

If you'd like to get really creative, try cutting and polishing the stones yourself. You'll need an angle grinder, a diamond cutting wheel, and a diamond polishing wheel (available at granite countertop suppliers and larger home improvement stores), as well as polishing compound. Cutting stone is simple—simply outfit the angle grinder with the cutting wheel and cut away, and always wear eye and hearing protection when cutting.

Polishing is just as easy. Outfit the angle grinder with a diamond polishing wheel, spread a thin layer of polishing compound over the stone surface, and slowly work the wheel across the stone surface until you achieve the luster you desire. Remember—you're not polishing stone to be used for a countertop in your home, so it's perfectly fine if imperfections and scratches show.

To adhere the sections of stone together, use concrete or thickset mortar. Mix it according to the directions on its package and trowel it between the individual stones. There's no rhyme or reason to how you stack your stones—simple create what looks good to you.

Metric Conversions

METRIC EQUIVALENT

RANGE 1/64 INCH TO 1 INCH												
Inches (in.)	1/64	1/32	1/25	1/16	1/8	1/4	3/8	2/5	1/2	5/8	3/4	7/8	1
Feet (ft.)													
Yards (yd.)													
Millimeters (mm)	0.40	0.79	1	1.59	3.18	6.35	9.53	10	12.7	15.9	19.1	22.2	25.4
Centimeters (cm)							0.95	1	1.27	1.59	1.91	2.22	2.54
Meters (m)													

RANGE 2 INCHES TO 39.4 INCHES												
Inches (in.)	2	3	4	5	6	7	8	9	10	11	12	36	39.4
Feet (ft.)											1	3	3 1/12
Yards (yd.)												1	1 1/12
Millimeters (mm)	50.8	76.2	101.6	127	152	178	203	229	254	279	305	914	1,000
Centimeters (cm)	5.08	7.62	10.16	12.7	15.2	17.8	20.3	22.9	25.4	27.9	30.5	91.4	100
Meters (m)											.30	.91	1.00

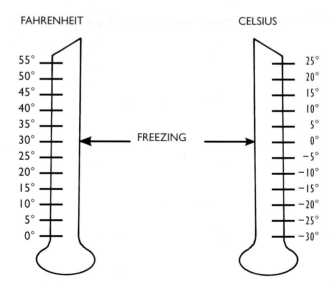

FAHRENHEIT   CELSIUS

55°   25°
50°   20°
45°   15°
40°   10°
35°   5°
30° ← FREEZING → 0°
25°   −5°
20°   −10°
15°   −15°
10°   −20°
5°   −25°
0°   −30°

CONVERTING MEASUREMENTS

TO CONVERT:	TO:	MULTIPLY BY:
Inches	Millimeters	25.4
Millimeters	Inches	0.039
Inches	Centimeters	2.54
Centimeters	Inches	0.394
Feet	Meters	0.305
Meters	Feet	3.28
Yards	Meters	0.914
Meters	Yards	1.09
Miles	Kilometers	1.609
Kilometers	Miles	0.621
Square inches	Square centimeters	6.45
Square centimeters	Square inches	0.155
Square feet	Square meters	0.093
Square meters	Square feet	10.8
Square yards	Square meters	0.836
Square meters	Square yards	1.2
Cubic inches	Cubic centimeters	16.4
Cubic centimeters	Cubic inches	0.061
Cubic feet	Cubic meters	0.0283
Cubic meters	Cubic feet	35.3
Cubic yards	Cubic meters	0.765
Cubic meters	Cubic yards	1.31
Pints (U.S.)	Liters	0.473 (Imp. 0.568)
Liters	Pints (U.S.)	2.114 (Imp. 1.76)
Quarts (U.S.)	Liters	0.946 (Imp. 1.136)
Liters	Quarts (U.S.)	1.057 (Imp. 0.88)
Gallons (U.S.)	Liters	3.785 (Imp. 4.546)
Liters	Gallons (U.S.)	0.264 (Imp. 0.22)
Ounces	Grams	28.4
Grams	Ounces	0.035
Pounds	Kilograms	0.454
Kilograms	Pounds	2.2
Tons	Metric tons	0.907
Metric tons	Tons	1.1

CONVERTING TEMPERATURES

Convert degrees Fahrenheit (F) to degrees Celsius (C) by following this simple formula: Subtract 32 from the Fahrenheit temperature reading. Then multiply that number by $\frac{5}{9}$. For example, 77°F − 32 = 45. 45 × $\frac{5}{9}$ = 25°C.

To convert degrees Celsius to degrees Fahrenheit, multiply the Celsius temperature reading by $\frac{9}{5}$, then add 32. For example, 25°C × $\frac{9}{5}$ = 45. 45 + 32 = 77°F.

List of Birds

Resources

Bird Watcher's Digest
P.O. Box 110
Marietta, OH 45750
800-879-2473
www.birdwatchersdigest.com

American Bird Conservancy
P.O. Box 249
4249 Loudoun Avenue
The Plains, VA 20198-2237
www.abcbirds.org

American Birding Association
P.O. Box 6599
Colorado Springs, CO 80934-6599
800-850-2473
www.americanbirding.org

Cornell Laboratory of Ornithology
159 Sapsucker Woods Road
Ithaca, NY 14850
800-843-2473
www.birds.cornell.edu

National Audubon Society
225 Varick Street
New York, NY 10014
www.audubon.org/bird/at_home/
HealthyYard_BirdHabitat.html

National Wildlife Federation
Backyard Habitat Program
11100 Wildlife Center Drive
Reston, VA 20190
www.nwf.org/Get-Outside/Outdoor-
Activities/Garden-for-Wildlife.aspx

The Nature Conservancy
4245 North Fairfax Drive #100
Arlington, VA 22203
www.nature.org

North American Bluebird Society
P.O. Box 7844
Bloomington, IN 47407
www.nabluebirdsociety.org

Photo credits

Brian Small: pp. 17, 23, 39, 45, 51, 67, 73, 97
Shutterstock: pp. 33, 61, 79, 85, 91, 103

Field Notes

HOUSE	TYPE, DATE INSTALLED, AND LOCATION	COMMENTS

Meet the Author

Michael Berger is a nationally recognized home-improvement and DIY expert and outdoor enthusiast. As a former editor for Popular Woodworking Books and *HANDY* Magazine, Mike has spent more than seventeen years teaching people how to successfully build projects and work with tools. When not in his shop, he spends his time either underground mapping cave systems, or underwater identifying and documenting historic shipwrecks.

Information and Projects for the Self-Sufficient Homeowner

WHOLE HOME NEWS

From the Experts at Cool Springs Press and Voyageur Press

For even more information on improving your own home or homestead, visit **www.wholehomenews.com** today! From raising vegetables to raising roofs, it's the one-stop spot for sharing questions and getting answers about the challenges of self-sufficient living.

- -

Brought to you by two publishing imprints of the Quayside Publishing Group, Voyageur Press and Cool Springs Press, Whole Home News is a blog for people interested in the same things we are: self-sufficiency, gardening, home improvement, country living, and sustainability. Our mission is to provide you with information on the latest techniques and trends from industry experts and everyday enthusiasts. Join us at **www.wholehomenews.com** to keep the conversation going. You can also shoot us an email at wholehomenews@quaysidepub.com. We look forward to seeing you online, and thanks for reading!